Peace, Mrs. Packard and the Meaning of Life

Peace, Mrs. Packard and the Meaning of Life

GARY LAUTENS

Introduction by Jackie Lautens

KEY PORTER·BOOKS

Canadian Cataloguing in Publication Data

Lautens, Gary
  Peace, Mrs. Packard and the meaning of life

ISBN 1-55013-518-X

I. Title

PS8573.A88P4   1993   081   C93-094231-0
PR9199.3.L38P4   1993

The publisher gratefully acknowledges the assistance of the Canada Council and the Government of Ontario.

Key Porter Books Limited
70 The Esplanade
Toronto, Ontario
Canada M5E 1R2

Design: Annabelle Stanley

Printed and bound in Canada

93 94 95 96 97 6 5 4 3 2 1

Contents

Introduction

What can you say about a man who revealed a part of himself every time he sat down before his trusty old Underwood?

As I read through the files of Gary's newspaper columns to make selections for this book, I felt as though I were having conversations with him. His phrases, pet peeves, sense of fun and wonder, likes, loves, and yes, his indignation and anger, are all there. What appeared on the pages of the *Toronto Star* under his byline, was exactly who Gary Lautens was.

Newspapers and the media have played a large part in the Lautens family history. Gary's father, Joe Lautens, worked at Canadian Press for fifty years. In those years, CP maintained offices, with teletype machines rattling out the news minute by minute, in newspaper offices across the country. Joe met his bride-to-be, Bertha George, at the *Winnipeg Free Press* where she was working in the circulation department. His job was to maintain the CP equipment in the *Free Press* building and to receive and send the news stories of the day for the news agency. They were married in August 1927. Shortly afterwards, CP transferred Joe to Fort William, Ontario. It was there that Gary arrived on the scene on November 3, 1928. Gary was exposed to printer's ink early in life. His father worked the nightshift while in Fort William, and Bertha used to take her baby son to the newspaper office at night to keep Joe company.

When Gary was two years old, his father was transferred to the *Hamilton Spectator* where Joe remained until he retired. Gary grew up in Hamilton. After graduating from McMaster University in 1950, he went straight into the newspaper business. For a little more than a decade, Joe and his two sons, Gary and Trevor, worked together at the

Spectator. In 1962, Gary left to join the *Toronto Star* and in 1963, Trevor left to write for the *Vancouver Sun*.

The media connection extends to other members of the family as well. Gary's cousin Morley Lautens was with *Time* magazine in Canada and New York, and is now with *People* magazine in Chicago. Morley's daughter, Karen, has branched out into television. Another cousin worked for *Cosmopolitan* and *Fortune* magazines.

Our two sons carry on the family tradition. Richard is a photographer at the *Toronto Star* and Stephen writes a column for the *Toronto Sun*. We keep trying to talk their sister, Jane, into seeking a position at the *Globe & Mail* so that we can have a family member on each of the city's major papers, but she appears to be reluctant. She did work at the *Star* one summer; however, her interests lie in different directions.

Football was a major item in Hamilton in the fifties. In 1950, the city's two major football teams, the Wildcats and the Tigers, had amalgamated to become the Tiger Cats. Hamiltonians loved their TiCats. I met Gary in the fall of 1956. I was eighteen and had just entered the working world. My father had played football for the Wildcats and he prompted me to enter the Miss Tiger Cat contest (remember, this *was* the fifties). Gary was twenty-eight, a sports columnist, and an organizer and judge of the contest. Another contestant and I tied for first place; Gary broke the tie by voting for the other person. About a week after the contest, he asked me out for dinner and a Leafs hockey game. We were engaged five weeks later and married less than six months after we first met.

Gary was an intriguing man to live with. For the nearly thirty-five years that we were married, it was never dull. He loved to plan surprises, go for long walks, travel to London once a year to see plays, and spend time at our cottage in the Laurentians. He planned individual time with each of our children and was involved in their lives and the lives of their friends. Unsuspecting companions were often subject to a gentle probe into their lives—our kids called it "The Interrogation." Gary liked songs with clever lyrics, loved dancers, saw at least two movies a week, disliked eating outdoors (bugs, you know), didn't like city driving but loved his Volvo (said it matched his personality), and he had an unerring sense of direction in any European city we visited but regularly got lost in Toronto. Although he had a computer at home, he always wrote his columns at the *Star* on an ancient Underwood typewriter. He didn't "stockpile" columns, but wrote each day for the next day's paper, and was forever worrying that he wouldn't come up with an idea for his next column—yet always did.

Gary kept close ties over the years with his alma mater, McMaster University in Hamilton, and served on various committees and boards. As an undergraduate, he spent a lot of time in the office of the *Silhouette*, the campus newspaper, which was situated in the basement of University Hall. He began as the sports columnist, then became the editor. Much to the consternation of the campus authorities of the time, he and his colleagues used to leave the newspaper office through the window because it was much quicker than taking the long walk down the hall and up the stairs to the front door. A parkette on the campus was dedicated to Gary's memory last year. It is situated behind University Hall, near that same window. A scholarship has also been established at McMaster in his name to assist aspiring journalists.

As you read through this collection, you will see that walking down Church Street to his office and observing life as he went provided much of Gary's "slice of life in the city" material. He was always interested in whatever was going on around him, usually seeing things that I or others would easily miss. Precisely because Gary enjoyed that walk so much, the family, with the cooperation of the Department of Parks and Recreation, has had a park bench placed on Church Street in his memory. It is at the corner of Church and Queen streets by Metropolitan United Church, which is the scene of a number of the columns included in this book. This is a companion bench to one placed in Hamilton's Gage Park by family friends.

Gary's gift for observation has been passed on to our children, although it finds expression in differing ways. Stephen, like Gary, has the talent to express it in writing and Richard can pick out the essence of a situation through a camera lens. Jane's powers of observation, on the other hand, led her to a degree in the field of science.

Gary felt that we were put on earth to enjoy and be grateful for what we had and to try to make the world a little better for those around us and for those who were coming after us. His view was that it was up to each person to take responsibility for herself or himself and that to blame something or someone else for your problems was a cop-out. Gary had a passion for all of life, but he was no Pollyanna. As you will see from some of the pieces in this book, he became extremely frustrated at people who were selfish, inconsiderate or couldn't see beyond themselves.

One of Gary's favourite themes was imperfect man or woman striving for perfection. He was often the main character of his stories. His wonderful self-deprecating humour is evident in the column entitled "Damsels in Distress!" where he attempted to be chivalrous in assisting two mothers with babies in carriages trying to get through a door at the same time. When things didn't quite go as he had planned, he prefaced his explanation with, "Alas, a funny thing happened on my way to immortality."

Sometimes while Gary was reading his column in the

morning after the paper had been thrown up on our front porch, I'd see him wince at how much he had revealed of himself in the words he had written the day before. He'd say how easy it was to pour out your innermost thoughts to a typewriter. It was as though he was almost forgetting that in doing so he was making himself vulnerable to the many subscribers who might read those words.

At other times he wondered if anybody was reading his "stuff," although when the *Star* took readership surveys, his column was always highly rated. Some journalists thought his column was too "soft." Gary's perception was that the newspaper's readers needed a break from the doom and gloom of everyday life; however, he never underestimated their intelligence. He felt that everyday human occurrences were just as important as the "hard" news and that a balance was required.

Gary was at the *Toronto Star* for almost thirty years. He worked with a series of managing editors, some who liked his material, some who didn't. He was executive managing editor for a few years in the eighties, but ultimately returned to his first love, writing his column. Gary had an abiding affection for the paper and felt privileged to appear in its pages. During this past year and a half, the *Star* has been very kind to the Lautens family, particularly with regard to the rights to Gary's columns. We thank them.

Although Gary had a loyal group of correspondents, human nature being what it is, more people wrote to complain about a point he'd made in a column or about a perceived grammatical error than to praise him for something he'd written. After he died in February 1992, I received an overwhelming number of letters from his readers. Gary would have been astonished at this outpouring. Many people said they'd wished they had taken the time to write to him. It seems that he touched many, many lives—people who identified with him, people who had families who grew up with stories of our family, people who agreed with his outlook on life.

The comments from these wonderful letters were truly appreciated by our family. Here is a small sampling:

> "He had a marvellous sense of humour and he also had the wisdom to know what really mattered in life."

> "What big Wallabees he left to fill."

> "I, like many others, probably felt that he was family."

> "His voice of cardigan-sweater-calm-and-wisdom gave us pause to reflect, often leading to a productive perspective in a confused world begging to be sorted out."

There were many requests in the letters I received to reprint a collection of Gary's columns. I want to thank Stephen, Jane and Richard for assisting in the production of this book, and for their love and support. With them, I am pleased to present this collection of columns taken from Gary's last ten or so years at the *Star*. Although many of his columns were based on family life, most of Gary's columns were written on other topics. It is some of these columns that have been brought together in *Peace, Mrs. Packard and the Meaning of Life*.

The words that follow were written by a very human, joyful, thoughtful, caring man. We hope they provoke a thought or two, produce a smile, or perhaps even make your day just a little bit better.

Jackie Lautens

1

Welcome to My Neighbourhood

Here's why I like living downtown

Recently we visited friends who have this very posh house—swimming pool, walk-in wine cellar, exercise room with sauna, a white marble bathroom with whirlpool tub, billiard room, a dining room big enough to seat 14 or more, a greenhouse . . . well, you know. It was huge.

Of course I was jealous, but not as jealous as I would have been a few years ago. In fact, if the truth were known, I wouldn't trade house-for-house.

The reason is location.

The handsome place is in the suburbs and I have no great hankering any more for quiet and green lawns and long car rides to work and all that sort of thing.

In 1976 we moved to downtown Toronto into a tiny place that would have been called plain old row housing 20 years earlier. Whenever our suburban friends see it, they get claustrophobic and immediately try to soothe us by pointedly mentioning, "Why this kitchen isn't a bit small!" or, "Isn't the front room, ah, cosy."

What they are really saying, of course, is, "How can you live in this closet?" and, "I wouldn't keep our dog in a space this small."

Yes, I understand. My suburban friend has a children's room (with padded bar, TV, etc.) that is larger than our entire downstairs.

But we have Toronto at our front door—literally.

Within five minutes, we can be at 10 movie houses; the subway is across the street; Maple Leaf Gardens is a 12-minute walk; if we want to bank Saturday morning we can; we can also get a Baskin-Robbins doubledip in three minutes; we can swim at a health club in four minutes.

Weather no longer is a factor in our lives, not much of one anyway. Storm, blizzard or whatever, we can get where we're going by foot, or public transportation.

A library of world class? Greek, Vietnamese, Japanese food? A car wash or five-minute lube rack? A hospital? University? They are all at our doorstep. I like that, and so does the rest of the family.

When we moved from our home in suburban Burlington with a 234-foot lot to one in Toronto just over 13 feet wide, we weren't sure we were doing the right thing.

Now, despite city traffic, building that always seems to be going on around us, sirens in the middle of the night, and an occasional wino reeling down the street, we would have it no other way.

Our back porch looks out on a dusty alley; getting a parking place in front of the house is almost impossible (as well as illegal during the week); our "garden" consists of a barrel of impatiens by the front door and a window box in the back; when we have a party with more than eight people, everybody has to stand.

But the house represents freedom. It is our servant not our master.

That doesn't mean we don't like to escape to the country now and then, or sit in somebody's yard admiring the roses; it doesn't mean we don't get slightly green at homes with more than one bathroom, a garage for the car and bicycles, and a kitchen big enough to open the stove door without somebody having to move into the dining area. Oh, no.

But when you add the pluses and minuses, we like our tiny, downtown house that provides shelter and the rest without making a lot of demands on us.

Years later I can say we didn't make a mistake by moving into the city. The only problem is, now we're spoiled.

Unless you want to keep chickens, why in the world

would anyone live north of Eglinton?

Talk about a long stroll— 14,625 miles

I am too pooped to write a column today. If I took a dipper of steroids, sigh, and hired Charlie Francis as my personal coach, I couldn't manage a paragraph.

The reason is my track record.

This morning, as I trudged to work, I started to figure out how much pavement I pound.

I walk to and from work every day. It is a round trip of 5 miles.

Or, 25 miles a week.

If you subtract holidays and time away from the city covering really important events (e.g. showing my daughter Paris), I suppose I do it 45 weeks of the year.

Or, 1,125 miles a year.

And I have been making the daily march for 13 years.

That totals 14,625 miles I've walked back and forth to work since moving to Toronto.

It is even farther in kilometres—23,546.

What makes me even more weary is the fact the 14,625 miles has been done on Church Street.

Sure, in madcap moments I sometimes detour down Bond Street. If I'm really brave (perhaps one or two trips home per week), I'll take Yonge Street.

But, by and large, my footwork is done on Church Street.

Has any Toronto street in the past decade and a bit been better traversed? Am I not the king of streetwalkers when it comes to Church Street, no giggles, please?

Hong Kong is a mere 7,410 miles from T.O., as the jet flies. In other words, if I didn't make my turn at the usual corner, I could have walked practically to Hong Kong and back, and had a nice new suit to show for it in the bargain.

London is a crummy 3,580 air miles away. My tootsies have done the equivalent of two round trips to Buckingham Palace on Church Street. Mind you, I would have seen only one queen if I had gone to London.

Even more devastating, my pedestrian effort would have taken me to Honolulu (4,592 miles) and back—and there again.

Is it any wonder I'm panting?

Can you blame my dogs for wanting to be put up on the nearest desk, especially the little piggies?

Look at it another way.

This newspaper pays 40.7 cents a mile when you use your car for office business. Certainly getting to the office is part of my job.

So, for 14,625 miles, I figure the *Star* owes me $5,952.37. I will take a cheque.

Of course, I'll never see the money. Some smart accountant will bring up the statute of limitations or claim part of the walking was personal.

Probably the media will now want to interview my feet, ask how many pairs of Wallabees I've worn out, if I will take off my socks for a saucy page 3 photo, what time I can be at the CBC for a "Journal" item on *Walking—Is It the Way of the Future or Is This Guy Just Plain Whacko?*

When I finally leave this business, I hope they rename Church Street after me.

Bunion Boulevard has a nice ring to it. Or Fallen Archway.

Anyway, no column today.

June 12, 1989

Green shoots quicken my pulse

Yesterday morning I saw something on Church Street that quickened my pulse and put the kind of gleam in my eye that's worth 30 days in any magistrate's court.

What caused me to lick my lips and make an animal sound deep in the darkest recesses of my vitals?

Was it a flash of lovely knee exposed by a naughty gust? Did I stumble on a box of money in small denominations, conveniently dropped from a passing Brinks' van by a butterfingered guard?

No, no, much better than that.

I was walking past St. Michael's rectory when I observed with my own eyes the tiniest tips of green shoots coming through the ground.

No doubt about it — these are living things, tulips, if I'm allowed a guess.

Do you realize that there may be a spring after all, that it isn't going to be winter forever, that we have all survived another season of blast and howl?

Yippee!

There are many ways I can tell spring is on its way to the inner city. The other day I saw some happy lads sitting on a bench at the side of Metropolitan United Church, tilting back a communal paper bag, the first outdoor cocktail party of the year to my sure knowledge.

Yonge Street, too, has broken out in a palm of panhandlers who try to establish eye contact so they can beg change and bills for their sisters' eye operations. A month ago they wouldn't have put a bare hand at risk.

Grit blowing down the streets, a souvenir of winter sanding; high school rugger teams holding their first workouts;

99-cent specials at the dry cleaners; mats in office lobbies actually drying up; letter carriers down to issue jackets and a cardigan; construction workers removing wool liners from hard hats; button sellers throwing back protective plastic from their street displays of merchandise. . . .

Oh, yes, very lovely.

But my ultimate barometer of spring in the downtown core is the flower bed at St. Mike's. It is more reliable than the spring tune-up special at Canadian Tire, the end-of-season ski packages offered by Collegiate, the line-ups at Baskin-Robbins for Easter Wabbit (or a similar flavour-of-the-month), or spinach quiche on the brunch menu at The Monks.

Of course, I'm lulled into thinking spring is actually here when offered a free vegetarian breakfast by somebody in saffron playing the tambourine outside the Eaton Centre.

Yes, it's easy to succumb to the temptation of accepting the boxes of unprotected grapes on the sidewalk at Kensington Market as a sure harbinger of spring.

Certainly the song of the robin perched on the roof of a Speedy Muffler outlet, or flying over a garbage truck on Monday morning pick-up, is a siren call for those of us who live in the crowded centre of town.

However, winter is never definitely over until a bit of green pops through in that totally frank and honest garden.

You notice I'm not one to jump the gun. I've watched city workers give fire hydrants their encouraging spring twist. I've heard the tennis courts at Ryerson come alive with the sound of muffled serves. I've watched young women blown away at Bloor and Yonge and sail into the sky (in the general direction of Cleveland) wearing strappy little spring shoes. I've looked at the photographs outside the Colonial of women who certainly wouldn't dress that way in January or February.

But I wasn't swayed.

I could watch a flasher zip out the fleece lining of his trenchcoat in preparation for spring business, and I wouldn't commit myself.

Those buds at St. Mike's are the ultimate sign.

Take it from me, spring arrived in downtown T.O. on March 12, at 8:45 a.m.

March 13, 1981

I just can't help gawking at the Big City

Your agent tries to pretend he is a big-city swinger—blasé, sophisticated, ready at a moment's notice to drink Coke Classic from some fast woman's slipper. Ultimately, however, I am always found out as nothing more than an imposter from Hamilton.

It isn't the cut of my bowling jacket that gives me away, or even my ignorance about the location of such Toronto landmarks as Hogg's Hollow, The Junction, downtown Scarborough, etc. I have been to North York on three occasions in my lifetime. I fake the rest.

No, what betrays me is my gawk. I am cursed with a gawk that has small town written all over it. For example, I was on the subway the other evening and a man got on our car. He was dressed like a woman and I gawked. I gawked at his high heels. I gawked at his frock. I gawked at his 5 o'clock shadow.

That's what we do in Hamilton—gawk.

The other morning I was walking down Church Street when I came upon what is referred to these days as a "bag lady." The woman was cursing a stream, and at full voice.

8

She unleashed a mighty kick at a chain link fence at Metropolitan United Church. She then proceeded to the Queen Street corner where she began choking a newspaper box.

Of course real Torontonians just kept walking by.

I gawked. I almost gawked my way into the side of a building because I was looking at the woman, not where I was going. In a small town, that's what you do when people choke newspaper boxes — gawk.

Later that same day I was walking up Yonge Street just north of the Dundas intersection where people in long white outfits were peddling incense sticks. It was 3:30 and the street was crowded.

One young man grabbed incense sticks out of the hawker's hand and kept walking. The person in the white outfit chased him and there was a shoving match, won by the young man who had grabbed the incense sticks.

Nobody paid any attention — except me. I gawked.

About halfway up the block (where I gawk when young women in tight dresses ask if you'd like a date) the young man tossed the incense sticks into the street. I gawked at that, too.

I gawk at the self-proclaimed "World's Rottenest Writer" who peddles his books on the street. (He has just moved south from Bloor–Yonge to near Queen Street.) I gawk at the teenagers with shaved heads who panhandle on Yonge Street near Isabella. I gawk . . .

Well, let me tell you about one of my most recent gawks.

The other night the missus and I were in bed when we heard a tremendous row in front of our house. We gawked out the bedroom window.

A police cruiser was up on the sidewalk, practically on our porch. Another was across the street.

And there were four officers with drawn guns surrounding a man with his hands in the air. Another cruiser pulled up.

The police told the man to put his hands on the cruiser roof. He didn't.

Instead, he moved a hand toward his pocket. An officer placed a gun at the man's temple and said he'd be shot if he didn't do as he was told.

Finally, the man's hands were pushed on the cruiser, he was told his rights, he was searched, his hands were handcuffed behind his back and he was driven off in a cruiser while four officers stayed behind to examine the Volkswagen Beetle their suspect had been driving.

I have worked in Toronto since 1962, but I gawked at the whole episode. So did my wife. Of course, she's from Hamilton Beach and gawks at anything.

April 23, 1986

Horrors! They're putting in a park

The city is putting in another park within a block of our downtown home and some of us are up in arms.

We're not sure we can stand a second green space with shade trees, a graceful water fountain and perhaps flower beds so close to where we live.

In fact, I'm thinking of taking up a petition asking that the park be paved over and a major skyscraper put in its place.

Perhaps one with an all-night doughnut shop.

As anyone who lives near a city park understands, they are just plain trouble. You don't finish laying the sod and turning on the water fountain before winos, glue-sniffers and people with wild eyes move in and take over.

Before you know it, strangers are washing their underwear in the decorative waterfall and sleeping on discarded mattresses behind the flowering geraniums.

Instead of a nice patch of concrete, or even what's left of what used to be a service station, you have a 24-hour Garden of Eden where the partying never stops.

The women in our district detour around the one park we have now because they don't feel safe in any sylvan glade with concealing profusions of greenery.

If they have to walk around a second park, they may never get home in time for supper.

At the rate they're greening our area, we may soon be surrounded by parks, and then where will we go for a walk, especially in the evening hours?

We will become virtual prisoners in our homes, surrounded by grass, smart white-wire benches, designer chess tables, goldfish ponds and unshaven galoots passed out under the Please Keep The Park Clean sign.

Before we go a step farther, I feel the city should take a survey and find out if some districts are getting more than their fair share of parks.

Our block, for example, has at least four recreation areas within easy walking distance where you can be mugged, assaulted, subjected to an insulting suggestion or just plain scared out of your wits by somebody holding a plastic bag to his nose.

It is my sincere belief we are at least two well-lit buildings and, perhaps, a crowded shopping area behind the downtown average.

Fortunately, the new park doesn't have a lot of vegetation in place yet. I think a person could sprint across it in less than 15 seconds if wearing the proper footwear, just under 10 seconds if there is no moon and you hear a moan from behind the steel sculpture of the grazing animals.

That's a small blessing.

What all this park-building will do to property values in our neighbourhood I hate to guess. Who in his right mind wants to buy a home practically next door to *two* quiet, secluded parks in the heart of the city?

If anyone is thinking of selling, I hope he or she is wise enough to wait till winter—and then tell prospective buyers the empty space at the corner isn't a park but a construction site where digging for a 55-storey insurance tower will start in spring.

Well, it could add $25,000 to the selling price.

August 17, 1988

Motorist in a blind rush to near-tragedy

As I write this, it is 10:30 Tuesday morning.

Two hours ago I saw a man come within a hair of being killed on the street. I am still shaken.

What makes it even more bizarre is the fact the man didn't see his own brush with tragedy and cannot describe the events that follow.

Let me explain.

I was walking down Church Street to work as I do most mornings. I was on the west side of the street when I reached the Charles Street intersection, where the Town Inn is located, if that helps.

There is a stoplight at the intersection and I turned to the left to look at the one-way traffic that proceeds westbound.

That's when I noticed a man walking on the other side of the street. He had a rust-coloured sweater tied around his waist and was being led by a German shepherd, a guide dog.

Yes, he was blind.

That's when it happened.

A big charter bus was parked (illegally) at the corner, so the dog could not see what was coming along Charles Street.

And what was coming along Charles Street, as I could see from across the street, was a white sedan under full steam, trying to make the light.

The motorist did not see the blind man step off the curb because of the bus.

The car reached the intersection just as the man and dog walked out from behind the parked bus.

It was a heart-stopping scene.

The guide dog saw the car when it was almost on top of him. He cowered and backed away instantly, wrenching the handle of his harness from the blind man's grasp. The blind man froze on the spot, not knowing what was happening.

The motorist swerved and braked, just missing the man and winding up in the intersection at an angle.

It was blood-chilling.

The blind man retreated to the curb where the dog slunk down, ears back, tail low. Presumably he was aware he had broken the rules by leaving his master's side.

By doing so, though, he had also saved two lives—his own and the blind man's.

Incredibly, none of the principals said anything to the blind man.

The motorist drove off.

The bus driver never left his cab.

And the blind man, guide dog back at his side, continued down Church Street, turning in at a drug store at Wellesley.

Why was the motorist in such a hurry? To make a deal? To shuffle papers at the office? To get to the next stoplight at

Yonge Street?

Why was the bus parked at the intersection? For a coffee-break? To save a few steps? To pick up five minutes on a schedule?

I don't know.

Perhaps there is no moral to this little story. After all, it has a happy ending—blind man and dog live, the motorist gets through that all-important stoplight, the bus driver picks up his charter as arranged.

Perhaps the point can be made that, like the blind man, sometimes it is just as well not to know the dangers we face.

But just maybe we should pause in the midst of busy city life and ask ourselves now and then, "What's the big rush?"

We never know what's waiting just around the corner.

September 8, 1988

Downtown church and tale of two soles

The other morning I noticed something strange in a tree on Metropolitan United Church property: a pair of yellow work boots hanging on a branch 10 feet above the ground.

Now there are weird things to be observed in the downtown core, but in my daily walks past the Church–Queen intersection I have never seen work boots in the trees.

Naturally, my curiosity was aroused and I have been trying to think of explanations for the unusual sighting.

This is my list so far.

Someone lost an election bet and, in attempting to jump over the tree, only made it halfway.

The General Council of the United Church (by a 276–195 vote) has decided to decorate its trees this Christmas with work boots instead of stars and tinsel.

Conrad Black was just putting his boots out early for Santa.

Somebody in the area missed a yowling cat at three in the morning with both shots.

Pigeons in the inner city have become more affluent and now wear work boots to keep their feet warm in the cold Canadian winter.

Some smart ad guy put the boots in the tree to get publicity.

Because of the cost of land in Toronto, the Old Lady Who Lived In A Shoe has decided to go condo.

k.d. lang was trying to get a kite out of the tree when her footwear got caught in the branches.

The tree was blown into T.O. from Hamilton by the recent earthquake.

Cardinal Emmett Carter and some of the other cut-ups at St. Mike's put the boots in the tree as a joke on their United Church neighbours.

The work boots in the tree are a modern sculpture and will be reviewed in the *Star* next week by critic Christopher Hume. (Title of the exhibit: Shoe Tree.)

The work boots are being tested by Mark's Work Wearhouse to see how they stand up to our weather.

While the work boots appeared to be empty, they were actually being worn by Stealth Man, an invisible pilot invented by Canadian scientists to fly America's Stealth bomber.

A working woman on Church Street threw the work boots into the tree when a customer refused to pay his bill for personal services rendered.

Cinderella has become a Punker.

A construction worker won a major lottery and tossed the boots into the tree as his way of saying, "I quit!" to the job foreman.

Patrons of the nearby Irish tavern held a shoe-tossing contest and the competition ended in a tie.

A sophisticated transient staying on a bench in the Metropolitan Church property left his boots up the tree overnight expecting them to be shined.

Okay, what's your explanation?

December 5, 1988

It's just annoying, but I paid TTC $2 for nothing

To write a really good column you should be mad. If a vein is sticking out of your forehead and your lips are thin as a pencil line, you're home free. They will probably put you on page one.

Unfortunately, today I am only annoyed so you know what follows will win no prizes in the National Press Awards. Sorry.

Saturdays we go to the St. Lawrence Market. We walk down (about two miles from our house), spend our money and then take the subway home.

By the time we exit, my wife and I are loaded down with at least three or four shopping bags each and look like a poster for the Shouldice Hernia Clinic.

On this particular Saturday we put our tokens in the TTC turnstile and staggered down to the platform at the King Street station to be greeted by the sight all subway travellers hate—crowds of people.

The trains were temporarily stopped.

That's what the voice over the P.A. system said.

I asked a man how long he had been waiting. He said 10

minutes or so. The trains weren't running when he arrived either, so I don't know how long service was interrupted.

We waited. Another announcement of the delay. More wait. No train.

Finally, my wife and I took a vote and by a 2–0 margin decided we couldn't wait any longer. We had a son waiting for lunch before going to work.

We went back to the TTC booth but the man in charge wouldn't give us our tokens back. It isn't company policy.

Pleading did no good. Pointing out we paid two tokens for a ride the TTC couldn't provide was useless.

Why didn't he tell us the trains weren't running when we went through his turnstile? That would have been the right thing.

I can afford two subway tokens ($2) but I don't like to pay for something I don't get.

Of course, it doesn't compare with the real troubles in the world. If that is my biggest problem in life today, I'm lucky.

Okay, you're right.

Still, I was annoyed.

We walked back up the subway stairs (with our load) and got a taxi in front of the King Edward Hotel.

This sounds silly but taxis are a luxury to me. I think it's my age bracket. My kids think nothing of hailing a cab to go a few blocks. Not me. I figure it practically has to be a birthday or something.

My mother once fell in downtown Hamilton and broke a major bone. She still took a bus home. That is the kind of thrift that runs in my veins.

Okay, we took a taxi.

It cost $6, including tip, to get ourselves and the groceries home.

Plus the $2 the TTC got for nothing.

My wife tried to make me feel good by saying the $8 total

works out to only $4 per person, which is just $2 each way to the market since we walked down.

It was a very good explanation.

If she hadn't said anything, I might have been mad at the TTC instead of just annoyed, and written a really swell column. Page one.

January 29, 1990

Big city women take such pride in dressing drab

A major change has taken place in women's fashion and I think our newspaper may have missed it.

Our fashion section is filled with tips on how a woman can look better and attract admiring glances when out in public.

But if my personal experience is any yardstick, women in Toronto today are more interested in dressing down than up.

It's not that they've lost interest in personal grooming and knockout outfits.

It's just they don't want the hassle that comes with the territory. Who needs leers, rude comments and unwanted advances any time, let alone at 8 a.m. on the way to work?

When my wife leaves the house in the morning, I invariably try to cheer her up by telling her how drab she looks.

"That coat is really baggy and nondescript," I might say. "Nobody will give you a second look."

"Thank you," she says, happy I have noticed her effort to blend into the scenery.

"The high boots with the white stains are a nice touch," I often add. "Unless somebody has an X-ray machine on the Yonge line, they'd never guess you have nice legs."

That kind of praise is almost too much.

"I'm wearing my mitts so no one will notice I have a wedding ring and want to steal it," she may add, having read a story in the newspaper that morning about pickpockets and muggers on the loose in city streets.

"If you just wear that wool hat that ties under the chin, I think you'll be totally city-proof," I remark if I'm on my toes. "That way only the tip of your nose will show."

She may then do one last twirl in the hallway.

"Is there any possible way some smart aleck on a street corner or on the subway will think I'm the slightest bit attractive or want to bother me in any way?"

"No," I vow.

My wife then goes back upstairs to put on bulky leg warmers for insurance.

That's how it goes in many homes these days in thought if not actual words.

Women have closetfuls of wonderful clothes, patterned stockings, imported blouses, strappy little shoes, smart sweaters and delightful accessories, but they wouldn't dare wear them on the street.

It will just bring them dumb remarks, stupid whistles and infantile woo-woos, or they could be accosted by drunk panhandlers, people who talk to themselves or someone in town looking for a bad time.

I suppose the annoyances go with a big city and there isn't much you can do about it, except wait until you're with friends before you put on the perfume and wear the skirt that is just above the knee.

But if the *Star* was on its toes, it would provide a weekly column on defensive dressing, telling Toronto women how they can look their worst when on the street or riding a crowded streetcar.

All women in T.O. want is a little inattention. Is that

too much to ask?

"He's drunk," I said, but my wife gave him a hand

I am trying to be a cynic, but it isn't easy with my wife around.

Let me give an example.

A few weeks ago the two of us were walking on Church Street. It was noon. A Saturday.

We had been shopping and our arms were full of groceries.

We were heading home.

As we approached the Wellesley intersection, we saw an old man.

He was crawling on the pavement.

It was cold. The pavement was wet. And he was on his hands and knees.

It's a busy intersection with a traffic light.

And he was trying to cross the road.

On all fours.

I just looked in amazement. So did several other people on the sidewalk.

"He's drunk," I said to my wife. "Or he's on something."

My wife didn't reply.

She left my side and went over to the old man. She bent over and talked to him.

The next thing I knew she was helping him to his unsteady feet.

"He's trying to get to the other side," she said. "He wants to go to the bank."

The next thing I knew we were practically lifting him across the road.

He wasn't drunk.

He wasn't on something.

He just wanted to cross the road.

We got him to the bank and he said he was okay. He could manage now.

"Are you sure?" my wife asked.

He said he was.

We waited until he was safely inside and then left.

End of story.

But you can see the dilemma.

Just when you think you are street-smart and city-wise, someone comes along and surprises you.

How can you tell the genuine from the fraud? How can you distinguish between the truly needy and the foolish?

Not long ago a sturdy youth in front of the beer store asked if I could spare some change. "Sorry," I said.

"I'll bet you are," he fired back.

Once I stepped in when a man was abusing a woman. He wound up chasing me down the street—and the two of them were arm-in-arm at the end.

We let a young woman in our house a few years ago when she banged on our door for help.

She immediately threw up all over our living room rug. Drunk.

How can you tell when your help is really needed?

I don't know.

I guess you have to take chances now and then. I guess you have to bend over and ask an old man if he wants help, even if appearances are suspicious.

People will help if they see genuine need. Maybe they get a special star in their crown if they do get fooled now and then.

Anyway, it's tough being a cynic with my wife around.

January 28, 1991

Kids' bird feeders prove kindness isn't fly-by-night

It is Thursday morning as I tap these words.

And I am smiling.

What gives?

Is my tuque too tight? Has my brain passed its use-before date? Are they using aluminum pots in the office cafeteria again?

Don't I know there's a war, a recession, and lots of other awful things going on?

Yes.

But I can't help it.

I was walking down Church Street about an hour ago and saw a sight that's made my day.

Hanging from a tree outside Metropolitan United Church child-care centre were five milk cartons.

Each had a side cut out and a tiny perch.

Yes—bird feeders.

Obviously the kids made them.

And, to make the birds feel more comfortable, they drew pictures on the cartons.

Some of the crayon even stayed inside the lines.

It was wonderful.

Remember when you made bird feeders as a kid and hung them on branches?

Isn't it good to know some things don't change?

City birds aren't exactly things of great beauty, especially at this time of year. On Church Street the best you can hope for are sparrows, starlings and a scruffy assortment of sooty feathers, all gray.

Nor can you expect a cheery song.

Downtown birds can't whistle. If they could, they'd whistle for cabs and head for the country.

Don't blame them.

If you had to huddle around a neon sign to stay warm and teeter on a power line with streetcars passing every few minutes, you wouldn't be any Pavarotti either.

But that isn't important.

Kindness is good to see anywhere, but especially downtown.

A couple of weeks ago I was on Yonge Street in the middle of the afternoon when I saw a security guard struggling with a wild-eyed guy outside the Eaton Centre.

The guy was fighting to get loose but the security guard held him by the scruff of the neck.

Finally, the man was pinned to the sidewalk.

Very wild.

Two things fascinated me:

1. Nobody paid much attention to the struggle.

2. The security guard who bravely refused to let go was a young woman of about 23. She was absolutely determined to hold on to the kicking, swinging, fighting suspect.

When you walk through downtown as much as I do, you see a lot of weird things.

But that's why I liked the bird feeders so much. What a happy contrast.

Maybe when the kids who built them grow up, they won't become generals who order bombing raids and brag about "kills" and "kicking ass."

Maybe they won't get involved in stupid street altercations over who will get to the next stoplight first.

Maybe they won't abuse kids, old people, women.

Maybe they'll always think about helping the less fortunate.

I hope so.

The world needs more of that kind of people.

Building bird feeders out of old milk cartons isn't a bad way to start.

February 22, 1991

Come for a visit—but take your trash back with you

Poor Toronto.

Nobody ever defends it.

Take the garbage thing.

It's okay for Kingston to haul away its garbage to Ottawa where, apparently, nobody will notice a little extra.

But Toronto can't.

Toronto has to take care of its own garbage. No shipping out.

Okay—but what is Toronto's garbage.

People come here from Barrie, Hamilton, Detroit, Oakville and all sorts of places.

They come here to work.

To see baseball games. To hang around bars and pick up dates. To go to the art gallery. To shop. To see the view from atop CN Tower. To attend classes.

They make garbage.

Is that Toronto's garbage exclusively?

If we're going to be fussy about who owns the garbage, maybe people from out of town should take the garbage they make back to their own communities.

This is how it might work.

As soon as you enter Toronto you'd be handed a big garbage bag. Any garbage you make while in the city would have to be placed in the bag and taken home.

You know—pizza crusts, bits of paper from the office, hot dog wrappers, watercress you didn't eat, old Kleenexes, Leaf souvenir programs, mufflers that have been replaced at Speedy, oil from service calls.

Even members of the provincial legislature would be required to gather up the stuff in their wastebaskets at the end of the day and take it back to their out-of-town ridings.

I know this sounds hard but it would be fair.

As someone who commuted to Toronto from beautiful Burlington-by-the-sea, which has no garbage crisis to my knowledge, I know I contributed to Toronto's present dilemma.

And I feel awful about it.

Some of my old torn-up columns, typewriter ribbons and bits of the gone (but not forgotten) '71 Chevelle are probably still heaped in a Toronto dump, visited only by sea gulls and NDP cabinet ministers.

Meanwhile, Burlington-by-the-sea remained pristine and virginal. You could eat off the streets of Burlington-by-the-sea.

Why not?

I was making my mess in Toronto those 10 years.

I blush.

Naturally, if people visiting Toronto have to take their garbage with them when they return to spotless suburbs, or bustling Buffalo, Torontonians should take trash bags with them when they travel.

If we go to Muskoka for a weekend to practise breathing, or to Edmonton to see relatives, we should bring back the litter we create along with the hotel towels and table lamps.

That way coffee grounds, citrus rinds and bones from the

chicken pot pie will wind up with the person responsible.

And in the community dump where they rightfully belong.

Isn't that proper?

Isn't that the NDP way?

Forget about personing the ramparts.

Let Toronto's cry ring out in the halls of Queen's Park—"Let's dump on them before they dump on us!"

It's so hard running a government.

April 17, 1991

Tiny mouse lives to squeak about Bloor Street rat race

It has become a tradition for this department to return from the cottage each summer with a mouse story.

One year it was about waking up in bed in the middle of the night and discovering a mouse crawling up my arm.

Another year I revealed (exclusively) how we trapped a mouse in a tin can and my wife forced me to release it unharmed about a mile down the road because she thought it was so darn cute.

And so on.

This year we returned without a single mouse sighting and I was afraid I'd have no mouse story to offer loyal *Star* readers. I knew how disappointed you'd be.

Happily, we've both been spared rodent interruptus.

I have my 1991 mouse story.

Strangely, what I am about to relate did not take place in faraway cottage country. It happened right in downtown T.O.

Sunday evening your correspondent and the lovely Jackie

(the missus) went for a little walk along Bloor Street to enjoy a quiet $2, gulp, ice cream cone.

It was around 8:30 in the evening and I was feeling blue about a lot of things, mostly about paying $2 for a lousy ice cream cone. (Okay, it was $4.19 for two cones, thanks in part to the GST that 92 percent of Tories think is wonderful.)

We were just in front of Holt Renfrew when my wife said, "Look, by the curb."

I followed her finger and there was a tiny mouse.

On Bloor Street.

I have walked Bloor Street 78,950 times (estimate) and I have never seen a mouse before.

I have seen millionaires, street beggars, people with tattoos, musicians, office workers, Tommy Smothers, protesters foaming at the mouth, smart businesswomen going to mergers, tourists looking for a cheap (ha, ha, ha) place to eat.

But I have never seen a mouse.

"What's a mouse doing on Bloor Street?" I asked my wife.

"Maybe it just came into some money," she replied.

Don't laugh.

Bloor Street is no place for a churchmouse, or any other cash-strapped, warm-blooded vertebrate.

We watched the mouse and, believe it or not, it was trying to cross Bloor Street to get to the corner where Creeds once humanely offered to relieve the rich of the awful burden of carrying around all that money.

Crossing Bloor Street in the middle of the block, through four lanes of traffic, is no simple challenge for any human being not on anabolic steroids.

But a teeny weeny mouse?

We were astonished. Amazed. I'd say dumfounded but I can never remember if there should be a "b" after the "m."

Here, though, is the happy ending.

The mouse (not two inches long, minus tail) darted back and forth and, when there was a break in traffic, dashed across the street. Safely. Cross my heart, that's what happened.

When last seen, the mouse was on the southwest corner of Bloor and Balmuto.

One possible explanation I can give is that *101 Dalmations* is playing down the block at the Uptown Backstage.

Maybe the mouse thought Mickey and Minnie had cameo roles in the Walt Disney classic and wanted to catch the last show.

Or, maybe the mouse was heading to Union Station to go on holidays. Maybe it had too much coffee. Maybe it's initiation week at mouse fraternities. Maybe the Pied Piper is in town.

Hey, I don't have all the answers.

August 14, 1991

CNE is still Ex-cellent — even on a senior's pass

I can't remember having a bad time at the Ex.

Isn't that something?

I started going in the 1940s — so this is my sixth decade of visiting the old fairgrounds.

Still not bored.

How could you be?

I've ridden elephants at the Ex, been lost at the Ex, carried kids home from the Ex, bought plush snakes at the Ex, eaten dozens of tiny donuts at the Ex, told my youngest not to blow his bullhorn in the ears of the people in front of us at the Ex. . . .

Once the Ex saved my career. My first summer as a general columnist at the *Star* (after years as a sports columnist in Hamilton), I was scrambling for something to write about, unlike now, of course.

So I went to the Ex practically every day. No tattooed lady, sword-swallower, pitchman peddling magic potato-peelers nor weight-guesser went uninterviewed in that August of 1963.

I was at the Ex so often in search of another 600 words, the horses held their noses when I walked through their building.

If I may borrow from C. Dickens, people tired of the Ex are tired of living.

This year it was just as much fun as ever. For one thing, it was a breakthrough year.

For the first time ever I asked for seniors' prices.

If you're over 60, the Ex lets you in for $2.

This year I decided to heck with pride and vanity. I admitted I was 62 and they let me in for the old fogey fee. What was disappointing was the fact they didn't challenge me or ask for proof of age.

I guess I didn't comb the hair over my bald spot as carefully as usual.

Highlights of the day?

Well, I enjoyed the Greek sandwich in the Food Building that dripped down my front, and the 25-cent iced tea.

My wife's top food experience was a plate of pancakes which she topped with ice cream from a cone I had half-eaten.

Jackie loves pancakes. When we got married, she ordered pancakes on our honeymoon morning.

I attribute our long marriage to a good start. Offer Jackie pancakes (or ice cream waffles) and she will follow you anywhere.

We watched the bungee jumpers (including one who got to the top and changed his mind), boxers, a man playing a harmonica. We visited the Saudi building, the McDonald petting zoo, a women's body-building competition, a fashion show in the Swiss pavilion. . . .

All for my lousy $2 admission fee.

How can you beat that—over five hours of wandering around, staring at people, looking at great stuff, some of which you can even afford.

But know my favourite moment?

It was in the Bravo Canada building where a chanteuse named France Gauthier put on a mini-concert. She sang some Edith Piaf tunes and then finished with one of my all-time favourite songs, "La Mer" by Charles Trinet.

It was a lovely surprise—typically Ex.

France had on a long dress. *Très élégant*, as suave guys like me from Hamilton say.

But when she walked, you could see what she had on her feet.

Blue sneakers.

Dreams and reality.

Just like the Ex.

August 28, 1991

My spirit's sagged since athletic couple took a hike

I'm a nosey person by nature and profession. The business I'm most interested in is other people's.

Right now, for example, I'm curious about a young couple I used to see walking down Church Street every morning just after 8.

I don't know their names, never spoke to them in my life, can't tell you much about them.

But for a long time they were part of my daily life even though they never knew it.

They are (my guess) late 20s, business people, very athletic. She was about the same height as he—around 5 feet, 10 inches. A handsome couple.

Very neat and well dressed.

He always wore a suit and tie, and carried an athletic bag as if he jogged at noon or did an exercise class after work.

And she, carefully groomed, wore smart suits but always Nikes or Reeboks on her feet.

They moved along at a good clip, treating their morning walk as part of a fitness program.

That's the picture.

I should mention they always held hands and chatted away as they moved down Church Street with purposeful stride.

They joined Church at Wellesley Street and walked down to King Street where they kissed, he turning west, she going one more block and turning east.

You see, I did pay attention.

But I haven't seen them for months now. They have just disappeared.

At first I thought they were on an extended summer holiday and would reappear in the fall when we all get back to business.

No such thing.

So where are they?

Of course, I have considered several possibilities.

The bleakest is that they have had a lovers' quarrel and gone their separate ways, he to Edmonton to start life anew with an oil company, she to New York City where she is successful but unhappy.

Perhaps they have agreed not to see each other for six months and date other people.

I don't accept that for a moment, however.

In my mind they are off on some round-the-world adventure dreamed of for years. They could be in Australia, running around Crocodile Dundee country and having the time of their lives.

Or they may have taken advantage of the Toronto real estate slump and bought their first home in some comfortable suburb, leaving behind Church Street and gritty downtown air.

They could even be expecting their first child.

Now, isn't that a better scenario?

Maybe they've won a big lottery, decided to move back to their old home town (where the people are friendlier), taken a new job on Eglinton Avenue with a big raise in pay . . .

There are all sorts of sunny possibilities so don't even think of illness or a split-up or anything sad like that.

All I know is I miss them and hope they are all right. I hope they are still in love. And I hope they are still looking at each other with that special light in their eyes.

I just wish they had told me they were leaving my life, or at least sent a note.

September 23, 1991

Gary, P.I. finds those lovers

About a month ago I wrote about a young couple I saw every morning on my way to work.

They held hands, chatted away to each other and paid little heed to the world around them on Church Street.

They were obviously in love.

But one day they were gone and I wondered what had happened. I missed them.

Months went by before I speculated on their fate—had they moved away, taken new jobs, broken up?

No need to guess any longer.

A few days ago they reappeared in my life and this time I left nothing to chance.

After the couple embraced and parted at their usual corner (Church at King), I caught up with the young man, identified myself and told him of my interest.

He was kindness itself.

His name is Karl. He's an accountant. He came to Canada from Dublin about 10 years ago.

And the woman?

Katriona (pronounced Katrina). His wife.

She's from Dublin, too, but they met in Canada. In Kingston where she worked as a nanny. Katriona was only 18 and after two years was ready to go back to Dublin.

Karl talked her into staying, "to give it a shot."

Two years ago they were married.

And, yes, she's an athlete (as I speculated). Gives aerobics classes. Belongs to the Y. So does he, which explains the gym bag he always carried when I saw them together.

Very handsome couple.

She's 6 feet tall (I guessed 5 feet, 10 inches) and could bench press almost as much as Karl.

But her real work is computers. She works with a company that does animation stuff and loves it.

So where have they been those missing months?

Karl said they went back to Ireland for a month to see relatives and friends.

When they came back to T.O., Katriona changed to her new job. That meant they left later for work.

And now for the really good news.

Katriona is pregnant.

So some mornings she doesn't feel like walking to work.

Put it all together and you can understand why our paths haven't crossed in months.

On top of that, Karl's sister visited from Australia and that threw off their schedule, too.

So now you (and I) know about the couple on Church Street.

Okay, let me do a little gloating now.

In that column a month go, I had this sentence as a possible explanation for their absence from my life:

"They could even be expecting their first child."

Please, no applause.

I'm a Scorpio and we have this gift.

In any case, I'm glad I finally had a chance to meet Karl and hear his story.

I'm delighted he and Katriona are going to have a baby.

I'm happy they're all right.

I hope they forgive me for barging into their life and ask them to allow me one more intrusion.

I hope they let me know when the baby arrives.

I'd like to send flowers.

It's the least I can do for all the pleasure they've given me as I watched them walk down Church Street, holding hands, and dreaming their dreams.

Isn't life wonderful?

November 4, 1991

2

I've Tried
Real Work

Summer of '41 started my career

An announcement:

I started in the newspaper business 50 years ago today.

On April 15, 1941, I walked into the *Hamilton Spectator* as their official baseball boy, salary $3 a week.

I was 12 years old and it was my job to post scores on a chalkboard and put them in the newspaper's final edition.

Can you believe it—50 years ago.

I tried to get a job delivering papers, but was rejected on the grounds I was too small.

So I was hired by city editor, Jim O'Neil, to work after school in the editorial department.

How could he refuse me after my mother sent me for the job interview in a suit and snappy fedora? I have pictures if you don't believe me.

My immediate editor on the final was a man named Bob Hayes, who had an English bulldog that could have passed as his twin, although the dog was better natured.

And the sports editor was Walter McMullen, who had only one leg and smoked cigars, which he usually placed in the middle of his wooden desk if no ash tray was handy, or was.

Gus McKenty was the managing editor and he sent me out for Camel cigarettes (in the soft pack) for which he tipped me 10 cents, "for another brick in your home."

Oh, that's all very clear. Ask me anything.

Only 10 cities had major league teams then—New York had three of them, Boston, Chicago, Philadelphia and St. Louis two each. The others were in Cleveland, Washington, Pittsburgh, Detroit and Cincinnati.

FDR (Franklin Delano Roosevelt to you youngsters in the crowd) threw out the first pitch to open the '41 season—a

3–0 Yankee win over Washington with Red Rolfe, Tommy Henrich and Joe DiMaggio as the stars.

Okay, I cheated on that bit.

I had to look that up.

The first game of the season was actually played April 14 with the full season starting the next day.

My favourite team was the St. Louis Cardinals and I thought I had the finest after-school job in the world.

During the summer holidays, I replaced the real office boys when they took vacations, receiving an additional $12 a week for a grand total of $15 a week from the two jobs.

Let me tell you, the cent candy flowed like water and I had a new baseball glove ($2.10) in no time flat.

I could even afford to see Abbott and Costello in *Buck Privates* at the movies and Hope and Crosby in *Road to Zanzibar*.

Since that memorable summer of '41, I have been hanging around newspaper offices on some excuse — three years as baseball boy, then campus correspondent, columnist on the university newspaper, etc.

It is probably the clearest case of arrested development you'll ever see.

Oh, I've tried real work.

Didn't like it.

I had part-time jobs in factories, delivering mail, digging wells, as a Saturday floor walker in ladies' lingerie in a department store, in the income tax department, boxing groceries at an A&P.

I think the problem was they weren't any fun.

Oh, I've wanted to strangle about 875 bosses — but I was never mad enough to quit newspapers.

So here I am, gulp, 50 years later, still minding other people's business, still looking for the right word, the magic paragraph.

And still not finding it.
Maybe I'll take the rest of the day off.

April 15, 1991

No glamour in any war for me after summer of '42

Old memories die hard.

Some never do.

It was the summer of '42. I was 13 years old.

And I had a summer job at the *Hamilton Spectator* watching over the Canadian Press teletype machines.

I got $12 a week to tear off stories as they came over the wire and deliver them to the editors.

The summer of '42. August.

I was watching over the teletype machines as they began to pour out the names of the casualties from Operation Jubilee.

Dieppe.

The names came in by the yard. The missing. The wounded. The killed.

The Royal Hamilton Light Infantry was a major player in the assault.

And I remember anxious wives and parents lined up at the front counter in the editorial room.

They were there to get news of their men, their boys.

There was no TV, of course.

So the newspaper was their link to what was going on, to what was happening on that sandy hell thousands of miles away.

Later the wives and families came to that same front counter with photos of the young men who wouldn't be coming back.

As I say, that happened nearly 49 years ago, but I still can hear the teletype clacking out the names, I still see the families standing by that counter.

So don't trust me when I write about war.

War lost all glamour for me those grim days in the summer of '42.

I have no stomach for it.

I watched the TV this week.

It seemed like coverage of a football game. We had the date the war was to be played. We had depth charts. We had diagrams of best plays. We had spirited coaches making rah-rah.

I just felt rotten.

They say it's necessary.

Just as they said it was necessary in Panama. And before that in Nicaragua. And before that in Grenada. And before that in Vietnam. And before that in Afghanistan, Tibet, the Falklands, Lithuania . . .

Maybe they're right.

I guess they'll cheer and say it's great if the game / war goes well. I guess important men will win elections.

But I only see losing.

War is about killing. If you kill more than the enemy kills, you win.

I don't want to see people killed.

Not our people.

Not theirs either.

There are ordinary folks with ordinary dreams in Iraq. They feel pain as we do. They care about each other as we do. And if the raids go well, many of them will die.

That is what war is about.

Not long ago my university inducted an athlete into its sports hall of fame. The athlete had a wonderful career at McMaster and, before that, at my old high school in

Hamilton.

His mother, now past 90, was there to accept the award. Her son, Charlie, died in his fighter plane almost 50 years ago.

I wonder what she thought this week.

I know I was suddenly 13 again and it was the summer of '42.

January 18, 1991

Show you care: hug a newspaper columnist today

We have Mother's Day. We have Father's Day. We have days to honour secretaries, the labour movement, old soldiers, lovers, Queen Victoria, St. Patrick, Jean Baptiste, Scouts, non-smokers.

Only one group has been left out: columnists.

Nobody has come forward to praise this hardy band of men and women. Not B. Mulroney. Not the candidates for the Liberal leadership. Not even the United Church, which has a good word to say about everyone.

No, columnists are the last ignored group in the nation. There is no home for them to go to when their writing days are over. They have no telethons. If there is a bumper sticker saluting columnists, I have missed it. No calendar is put out each year featuring a columnist of the month.

Do politicians pass million-dollar relief bills for columnists when their supply of words runs out? Does John Crosbie defend columnists in the House of Commons?

Is there a lobby group fighting to exempt the columnist's tools — pad, pencil and 1947 Underwood — from the GST?

Ha, ha!

Nobody is exhorted to take a columnist to lunch, buy a columnist a flower or send a columnist to camp.

It is too much.

As the first step in recognizing these valuable members of society, I have prepared a short list on the care and treatment of columnists.

Here are some simple rules:

Columnists may say they don't mind criticism that is constructive. It is a lie. They don't like any criticism. They like praise, even if it's insincere.

Never invite a columnist to speak at a church meeting, club function, wedding reception. Most can barely ask for a fill-up at the service station.

When you meet a columnist, pretend he is much younger looking than his or her picture in the paper. It makes them happy.

Never tell a columnist how much you like another columnist's work. This really drives them nuts.

Don't blame the columnist for what else is in the paper. Columnists don't agree with anyone, especially publishers, editors, business analysts, cartoonists, the horoscope feature. They seldom agree with themselves either.

Don't feed columnists tin cans through the bars as they are on restricted diets.

Suppress the whim to ask a columnist where he or she gets ideas. If they knew where to get an idea, they would be out that very moment buying one with their Visa card or a bum cheque.

Don't send stories written by your cousin to the columnist for appraisal. It is hard enough for a columnist to convince the editor to run his stuff let alone somebody else's.

Adopt a foster columnist and send him your photograph, food parcels, sweaters and the keys to your winter place in Florida with a map showing how to get there.

Finally, don't ask the columnist what else he or she does besides write the column. Columnists also don't like to answer questions about expense accounts, how many hours they actually spend in the office and how they manage to get a trip to Paris every year.

There you have it—the 10 commandments of columnist care.

Maybe we could declare a Columnist's Day in February. If it gave Canadians a long weekend, I think they'd buy it.

February 5, 1990

Bloody Mary spoiled my lunch with boss

The other day one of the big shots at the newspaper invited me to his club for lunch. Of course, I was on my best behaviour. Even wore a necktie.

When you write the way I do, you can't have too many friends in the executive boardroom.

But on my way to curry favour and grovel, something went terribly wrong. In fact, it is now extremely doubtful I will ever become even semi-chairman of the board.

Let me tell you my sad story.

We sat at a table in the middle of the quiet dining room and, if I do say so myself, I was about as charming as I ever get. Oleo, to coin a phrase, wouldn't melt in my mouth.

I thought everything was wonderful—the weather, the menu, the carpeting, the view out the window, etc.

And then the waitress brought our drinks—white wine for the Big Cheese, orange juice for me.

That is when the luncheon went down the bathroom plumbing.

As the waitress reached over with our drinks, a drink on her tray began to slide, slide, slide.

It went over the edge and poured on my crotch.

Yes, I was drenched from waist to knee. Not only was I dripping, I was dripping Bloody Mary.

Have you ever had a Bloody Mary poured over your lap during an important lunch with your boss, especially when you were wearing a summer suit?

It is not a pleasant experience.

The poor waitress was horrified, of course. She immediately grabbed a napkin and made a beeline for the wet area.

I know her intentions were honourable, but whenever a stranger makes a lunge at that part of my person, especially in a public place, I get very shy.

"No need to wipe me off," I said, backing away from her friendly but (in my opinion) ill-conceived attempt to help. "It's just a gallon or two of Bloody Mary."

By this time, everyone in the sedate dining room was watching the man with the wet crotch.

Someone rushed over with a bottle of soda water brought from the kitchen. "This might take out the stain," she said.

I kept backing away. I did not want her help scrubbing the Bloody Mary either, not while wearing same Bloody Mary in the personal vitals.

With only vestiges of panic, I suggested everything was fine and that we should continue with lunch. Forget my dripping loins, I said more or less.

We were moved to another table while the little Bloody Mary that had escaped my front was cleaned up. Somehow, though, the lunch had lost a lot of its magic.

It is difficult to carry on a serious conversation with a boss while your crotch is squishing every time you so much as butter a bun.

About an hour later the Bloody Mary had dried and my

trousers had stiffened. The stain came just short of the knee.

The maitre d' didn't charge for the drinks and gave me his card with instructions to send him the cleaning bill for my formerly light blue suit.

Give my luncheon host credit, he only laughed out loud two or three times during my encounter, but the worst was yet to come.

On my stroll home up Church Street after lunch, I had to walk past several gentlemen who from the look in their eyes were ready to kill for a gulp of my suit.

May 25, 1987

Why I will remember Brian forever

Confession is supposed to be good for the soul. That is the only excuse for today's column.

Recently I got a telephone call from a young man named Brian wanting some information.

"Perhaps you'll remember me," he said. "I visited you in your office a couple of years ago and . . ."

Brian didn't have to say another word.

I remember Brian.

If I live to a thousand, I'll never forget that first meeting. Nor, I suspect will he.

For me it was one of the most scary, embarrassing moments of my life, one that still makes me squirm in discomfort.

Let me go back.

A couple of years ago, I got a call from Brian, whom I had never met. He said he followed the column and would like to meet me.

I agreed.

Brian arrived on time and I discovered he was blind. Apparently others read my column to him.

Of course I was flattered—flattered that he would come all the way to the *Star* to meet me, flattered he would have my paragraphs read to him on a regular basis.

So we had a grand old chat, discussing matters that now escape me.

When it was time for Brian to leave, I insisted on calling a taxi for him.

I also insisted on personally taking Brian through the various corridors to the elevator and to the very door of the cab.

Getting out of a big building can be a problem for the sighted, let alone the sightless.

Besides, I did not want anything to mar his visit.

The truth was, I was touched by his interest and didn't want to let him down or disappoint him.

We walked to the elevator, Brian gently touching my arm with his hand for guidance.

We went to the ground floor.

I escorted Brian through the main hallway.

I took him through the complex of doors.

I took him outside.

And then, God forgive me, I walked him right off a flight of concrete steps.

One second he was beside me; the next, almost like a comic strip panel, he was suspended in mid-air.

And then, he crashed down.

Don't ask how I could be so stupid. We were talking. I was so accustomed to walking down those stairs, it was automatic with me.

I didn't even think to mention what was obvious to me.

Brian was in a heap at the foot of the steps.

I thought I had killed him.

But he got to his feet while his "guide" apologized 300 times and asked if he was all right.

Brian kindly made a joke of it and I finally got him to the safety of the cab and away from my "protecting" presence.

I couldn't work the rest of the day. And I didn't tell the story, even to my wife, for days. It was too upsetting.

Remember Brian? Only forever.

February 25, 1985

Why I hope you don't have my number

Please don't telephone me.

Send me a letter, slip a message under my door, throw a bottle with my address in the nearest ocean, hire a skywriter, paint words on the family turtle, rent a mime, parcel-post a parrot with a paragraph committed to memory, order a Cookiegram.

But don't telephone.

It is not that your voice would jar me from deep thought about Meech Lake or free trade.

It is not that I am shy or have laryngitis.

It's this darn telephone.

For years I was perfectly able to handle a telephone. It rang. I picked it up. I spoke. You spoke. It was very simple.

But months ago this newspaper went really modern in the telephone department and got all this fancy equipment. All right, it's well over a year now.

I know, I should have mastered it by now.

But it drives me crazy.

Instead of a simple black device with one end for my ear

and the other for my mouth, I now have a console, a communications system, an electronic breakthrough.

I have buttons that read (from top to bottom): rls, conf 2, call trans, call fwd, speed call, i/c, msg center, plus two numbers, not to mention an * and a # plus numbers from 1 to 0.

Don't ask me what they mean.

Do not tell me what they mean.

I have enough junk stuffed in my head now without adding a lot more. All I want to do is make a call and, if it's a nice one, get one back now and then.

I do not want to take a technical course on anything that requires more talent than lifting it up and saying, "Hello."

As far as I'm concerned, that's all a telephone should do.

I don't want to be able to talk to 18 people in 18 different places at the same time. I don't want to take a second call when I'm already talking on the phone. I don't want to do a "#" on the phone, whatever that is, or even vol up or vol down.

Why do technicians, scientists and other university graduates at the Bell insist on complicating my life?

Just a few minutes ago a nice lady called with an advertising complaint. I told her she should talk to somebody else at the *Star*.

Do you think I could figure out how to transfer her to the proper party with just a few simple touches of the easy-to-use Bell push-button panel?

I could not. I finally told her to call back and ask somebody else.

I know—you think I'm dumb.

I can't argue the point.

Personally, I think people in white smocks have too much time on their hands. They are always tinkering in their labs and reinventing things that work just fine—clocks, typewriters, record players, stoves, cars, etc.

As a result, most of us go around totally bewildered by digitals, word processors, VCRs, microwaves, automatic chokes and so on.

Well, I draw the line at telephones.

I refuse to relearn how to use the telephone.

If Bell wants to complain, they had better have a postage stamp.

January 25, 1988

Life at your favourite daily is "just ducky" these days

It grieves me to report routine on the sixth floor at your favourite daily has been shot all to heck.

Usually, of course, we are a well-oiled machine, efficiency in motion, a thing of beauty, etc.

Not this week.

Our efforts to produce a bigger and better *Star* for readers have been disrupted by a family of ducks.

I should explain my office is on a floor inhabited by glinty-eyed accountants, tough executives, secretaries who care only about the newspaper in your hands—and lovable me.

Daily we toil, scarcely looking up from our labours, dedicated only to your reading pleasure.

But a few days ago a lovely mallard took up residence on the gravel roof outside my window.

Some hours later she emerged from under an air ventilator mount with three little ducklings in tow.

Yes, we have neighbours.

Since that moment our staff has been acting slightly

goofy as we watch mother and family parade around the roof.

Bean-counters are forgetting to count their beans. Execs are staring out windows when they should be standing on someone's neck.

Female staff members are oohing and ahhing as the feathery matriarch marches her little brood back and forth.

Even I, famous for my powers of concentration, have been distracted from the usual chores—saving the nation, trying to figure out (without taking off my shoes) how many more columns before holidays.

Instead, I'm watching a baby duck try to get over a steel beam that separates him from Mom.

Oops, there he goes.

We have called experts who reassure us the ducks will be okay on the roof. We have put a little dish outside for water.

We have considered giving our newborn names— something like Huey, Dewey and Louie, or Curly, Larry and Moe.

(We look with less favour on an accountant's suggestion we name them Profit, Market Share and Bottom Line.)

In short, we have become foster parents.

Instead of coming into the office and asking, "What's the price of gold on the Tokyo exchange?" or "How about that Boris Yeltsin, eh?" our first question of the day is, "Are they still there?"

Nobody has to ask who "they" are.

We also hold long discussions on how the mother duck feeds the babies, since she never seems to leave their side.

If she is flying off to the lake across the street and returning with a beakful of goodies to regurgitate into the throats of her children, we have not seen it.

And we have seen no sign of a father helping out. (Attention, Life section: there could be a scolding comment from an NDP spokesperson on lack of affirmative action in the bird world.)

In any case, it's wonderful to watch new life and think about Nature and all its beauty.

In the meantime, forgive me if I make a spelling mistake or throw your morning paper in the bushes.

I'm up to my ears in ducks.

June 14, 1991

Jesus changed the water, but media just make whine

Okay, Brian is right.

The media can get pretty gloomy. Our motto is, "A day without sunshine is a terrific news day."

Of course, I'm crazy to admit I side with B.M. the P.M. over anything.

Look, according to the last figures I saw, his approval rate in Ontario is 8 percent.

That means 92 percent of readers immediately get steamed if a scribbler says anything good about our leader.

After all, Brian will go down in history books as the man who de-industrialized Canada. His idea of cleaning up the environment is shipping our factories to the States.

So he's not perfect.

But he does make a point about the media. Eliminate sex, violence, conflict and the Maple Leafs from the news and all you have left is the horoscope column.

That, however, is life (so we claim).

For example, I wonder how a media person would have handled the story if he or she had been present when Jesus turned water into wine at the wedding.

My guess is the story would have read like this:

"While in attendance at the nuptials of a young couple yesterday, Jesus of Nazareth, a carpenter by trade, turned water into wine.

"Some wedding guests were astonished but in this reporter's opinion the wine lacked nose and was too fruity to be truly impressive.

"It also was from an indifferent year—perhaps 25 or 28 A.D., not vintage years for claret.

"If Jesus had produced a nice dry champagne, it would have been far more acceptable for the wedding toasts.

"As it was, however, only the most generous of critics would consider it anything more than plonk. And domestic plonk at that.

"Let us hope Jesus does better the next time he turns water into wine and offers a wider selection, perhaps a saucy chablis. Wine producers in Gaul have nothing to fear from the local vintner."

Or let us go farther back in history to the moment when Moses parted the Red Sea.

A columnist with the *Mount Sinai Gazette* would have taken sharp stick in hand and commented:

"Leading a band of followers through the desert this week, Moses, the man who claims he talks to burning bushes, parted the Red Sea for his followers.

"Spectators applauded his baffling performance, certainly a breakthrough in the entertainment world.

"But one couldn't help wondering if a career can be based on what is basically a one-trick performance.

"Put another way, how many times can you watch a sea parted without getting bored?

"This is 1200 B.C. Audiences are sophisticated. Even with promotion, sea-parting has limited appeal. Moses needs an opening act, perhaps a comic to lighten the mood,

51

maybe an orchestra.

"Granted, he's got a great finish, but this reviewer can only give one thumb up. If you're into awe and spectacle, this is a show for you, but if you're lukewarm about aquatic acts (like yours truly) and want some laughs, give it a miss."

Yes, Brian isn't all wrong.

We can be pretty critical in this business.

December 4, 1991

Twenty depressing things that drive all writers nuts

According to a 15-year study reported in *Psychology Today*, writers are four times as wacko as other people.

Yesterday's *Star* revealed: "The study found 43 percent (of writers) had some degree of manic-depressive illness compared with 10 percent of a comparison group matched for age, education and sex."

The skimpy story did not give our side of it.

Herewith are 20 things that depress writers:

1. Trying to find a sharp pencil around the house and a piece of paper that isn't all covered with telephone doodles when you finally get an idea, or one that will pass as an idea in dim light.

2. Getting a letter from a reader filled with all sorts of flattering praise and then finding out near the bottom that it's praise for something somebody else on the paper wrote.

3. Not knowing what the green bits are in the office cafeteria's Chinese special du jour.

4. Converting to a word processor after years of working a faithful typewriter that didn't lose your entire story if you happened to hit one wrong key, which everyone does,

especially if he only uses two fingers lik3 th9s.

5. Reading that some other writer is getting $400,000 for writing a movie script that features Kim Basinger in garters.

6. People who disagree with you.

7. The knowledge that while you are trying to solve major problems in the world the sports writers are down in some sunny place getting tans and pretending to know and care whether the Blue Jays will have left-handed pitching strength this season.

8. Getting the carbon paper in backwards.

9. A spouse who reads your stuff and doesn't double over with laughter immediately and say this is the best stuff she has ever read in her entire lifetime.

10. Nit-picking editors who expect you to have an explanation for the "incidentals" entry in your expense account. These people are heartless.

11. People who won't drop everything immediately when you telephone them for important information.

12. People who expect you to drop everything when they telephone you for some silly reason.

13. All research, which is really boring.

14. Countries that keep changing the names of their capital cities and then expect you to know how to spell them. I mention no names but one of the worst offenders is that big country in Asia, you know, the one that is sort of off to the left when you look at British Columbia, and up a bit.

15. Readers who send you pictures of their cats.

16. Leaning back in your chair to get an idea and then toppling right over. It is especially depressing if you have visitors and are trying to impress them.

17. TV anchormen who get about 100 times more money and always have hair.

18. Trying to decipher notes you have written to yourself

and not being able to make out a word of what you considered a brilliant idea at 3 a.m.

19. Family members who think you should stay home for the repairman because you are only going to be writing, which isn't important like going to an office or aerobics class.

20. *Psychology Today* articles about writers being nutso. I would punch them on the nose if I didn't have my thumb in my mouth.

March 25, 1987

Jack's been poor, Jack's been rich, and guess what...

I've probably asked more questions than just about anyone in T.O.

It goes with the job.

I've asked Helen Gurley Brown about sex, Mickey Mantle about curveballs, Malcolm Muggeridge about death, Esther Williams about swimming, Eisenhower's doctor about heart attacks, E.P. Taylor about racehorses, Jean-Claude Killy about skiing, Pierre Trudeau about politics, Gordie Howe about elbows . . .

But the dumbest question I ever asked was a question I asked Jack Kent Cooke.

I still cringe when I think of it even though it was over 25 years ago.

Cooke, of course, is hot news again this week because his Washington Redskins football team is playing in the Super Bowl against the Buffalo Bills.

Undoubtedly we'll see the 79-year-old billionaire in dressing room shots if the favoured Redskins win the game.

I'm glad I'm not there to interview him. He might remember the dumbest question he was ever asked and have security eject the guilty party—me.

This is how it happened.

I was doing a radio show in Hamilton on CHML. Each day I telephoned someone interesting and had a chat.

I talked to Chester Gould who conceived Dick Tracy. I talked to Agatha Christie (briefly) at her home in England. I talked to Mel Torme about the death of Nat (King) Cole. I talked to Lorne Greene, Judy Garland, Dr. Jonas Salk.

One day I got the bright idea of calling Cooke.

There were problems: I didn't know Cooke. Cooke was a very busy man. The show didn't pay guests a dime. And it was spur of the moment.

We had only one card up our sleeve.

We were calling from Hamilton and that's where Cooke was born.

Sure enough, the tycoon took the call.

For the first few minutes it couldn't have gone any better. Cooke called me Gary and was delighted to have a chance to talk to the good people of his native city.

Then came my bomb.

All I can say is, I was young. I was naive. I was stupid.

I asked Cooke: "Is rich better than poor?"

I don't know what I was driving at. I think I expected him to recall wonderful days in his youth when he sat around the simple family table, eating beans and playing with a stick found in the mortgaged yard.

Or five-mile walks to one-room schoolhouses where happy children had to share a single crayon and do arithmetic problems on the faces of classmates for lack of paper.

Or the laughter that comes from watching the antics of an imaginary family dog as it cavorted in the snow piling up in the bed shared by the entire family on Christmas Eve.

I don't know what I expected but I got a very ominous pause and then Cooke's reply.

"Of course rich is better than poor, you darn fool. What kind of stupid question is that?"

I remember little after that.

The conversation limped on for a few more minutes but not even nostalgia could save the day. Cooke obviously felt he was dealing with a world-class boob.

Our paths, ahem, haven't crossed since that day.

I hope Jack Kent Cooke's team wins Sunday.

And I pray no young reporter comes up to him afterward and sweetly asks, "Is winning better than losing?"

Cooke could kill this time.

And not even Judge Wapner would convict him.

January 24, 1992

My beloved Underwood typewriter suits me to a "T"

Your correspondent is still shaken. Last week I almost lost my best friend at the newspaper.

My typewriter.

When I joined the *Star* in 1962, I was assigned typewriter 579. An Underwood.

At that time it was 12 years old.

Since then I have worked on nothing else at the office. Every word you've ignored from these veteran fingertips has been tapped out on typewriter 579, 42 years old next birthday.

We are more than a team.

We are buddies.

I'm the only scribbler at your favourite daily who toils

exclusively in this building on a manual typewriter.

The rest use computers.

But no fair-weather friend I.

I still have the Underwood portable I used as a student columnist. It was made in the 1920s and bought for me by my mother from a salesman who assured her in 1948 it had only been used Sundays in the previous quarter-century by a sensitive minister for sermons.

I do not follow whim or trend. If something works, I stick with it.

But back to my brush with tragedy.

In the middle of a column last week, my typewriter began to act funny. I, of course, blamed the flu—of which so much seems to be going around these days.

After faltering in a sentence or two, typewriter 579 sighed —and threw a key.

The "T" key.

As you know, all keys are important but the "T" key is one of THE most vital after the vowel keys.

Try to write something as simple as, "The Tories should scrap the GST and free trade pact" without a "T" key.

What comes out is, " he ories should scrap he GS and free rade pac ."

It is my belief a person cannot save the free world without a "T" key.

It is top priority.

Or, " op priori y" as I was typing in my moment of anguish.

Because of my problem, I was forced to borrow some new-fangled device called the electric typewriter to finish the column I had in progress.

It was awful.

I triple-spaced, I goofed spellings, I got my margins all wrong. You can't even bang at those electric typewriters without getting a bunch of letters you don't want.

"Brian" comes out "Brrrrriannnn" if you aren't really careful.

Naturally, I put in an emergency call for the repairman who, every July when I'm away on holidays, services my typewriter, asks it to cough, and puts in a new ribbon.

He couldn't make it for 24 hours!

Of course, I went the entire 24 hours without typing another word. Why attempt it? Without #579 I am verbally challenged, as silent as a tongueless statue, an end table.

During the 24 hours, I thought up ways to end the fighting in the Middle East, solve our recession and make Quebec smile like a cat on a cream route. I think I also had a surefire way to improve Leaf scoring.

But, of course, all of it went down the drain.

No typewriter. No column.

The part I needed to resume my career cost 20 cents.

It isn't cost that worries me.

It's manual typewriter technology.

When the last Underwood mechanic calls it a day, I'm out of here. Typewriter 579, too.

I refuse to share a career with anything that has to be plugged into the wall.

January 20, 1992

Loyal *Star* reader Marge Mundy is Number 1 in a million

The *Star* you're holding will be read by about a million people.

Of course, they're all people of intelligence, taste and sweet disposition.

But my favourite *Star* reader is Marge Mundy.

I've never met Marge Mundy. I've never seen a photograph of Marge Mundy. Marge Mundy and I never went to the same school, church nor Hamilton lunch counter.

Still, she is No. 1 with me.

Marge Mundy writes me two or three times a week.

The letters are in her own hand, usually three pages long and always signed, "Peace, love and blue skies."

Cruel winter, hot summer, during vacation, boom times and bust, Marge Mundy's letters arrive at the office.

They offer opinions on everything under the sun—Brian Mulroney, Quebec, American presidents, social conditions, immigration, court cases, the Leafs, sex.

Sometimes Marge Mundy encloses clippings with comments in the margins. Sometimes she underlines things I've written with opinions like, "har, har," or "I agree" or just a simple "!!!"

I have never had a more loyal reader.

All I can tell you about Marge Mundy is that she is a grandmother, a widow, lives in a Scarborough apartment and wouldn't vote for Brian if you could skate in hell.

Our relationship has been going on for years and not even the cost of postage stamps has slowed down my mysterious pen pal.

It's surprising what readers write about.

If I asked you what recent column attracted the most mail, I'd bet $5 (cash) you couldn't guess—even with three tries.

It was a column about a Knowlton Nash Christmas Party.

In the column I made a grammatical boo-boo.

I wrote about Knowlton "inviting Sen. Davey and I" to the same luncheon.

Of course, it should have been "me"—not "I."

I would blame it on drink, but I don't drink. I would

blame it on bad upbringing, but I had a good upbringing.

Let me just say I was overcome with brain fever or suffering from an overdose of red jujubes.

Anyway, that goof attracted mail from as far away as Sackville, New Brunswick. I got 25 letters ranging from deep hurt to outrage. How can I expect to run the world when I don't even know my English from a hole in the ground?

The record amount of mail from one column still is held by a 1978 piece I did.

A friend of mine, Mel Lawson, had a lovely foal in his racing stable and I asked readers to pick a name for the little fellow.

I got 17,000 letters. Approximately 95,000 names were suggested in those letters. And we had to hire people to open the envelopes to make it easier for Mel to look at every single suggestion.

(The winning name was Misty Mogul and the horse, alas, did not grow up to have a stellar career at the track.)

In any case, Marge Mundy hasn't quite reached that record as a correspondent.

But if I write long enough, I'm sure my faithful reader will come darn close.

Peace, love and blue skies, Marge Mundy.

January 27, 1992

3

Peace, Mrs. Packard and the Meaning of Life

In the name of peace...

With all the war talk in the newspaper this week, I've decided to do something controversial—a peace story. At the risk of offending the pro-war lobby, I've jotted down some of the nice things about peace.

Peace is quiet. Peace doesn't cause bleeding.

You don't have to wear a prickly uniform or go around saluting somebody you don't like to wage all-out peace.

Peace doesn't blow the roof off your home or make deep holes in the road.

Peace is considered a very good environment for raising children.

Peace lets you spend Saturday night at home watching the hockey game on TV, or sitting on the chesterfield in the front room kissing somebody you like.

You can wear flowers to peace.

Peace doesn't make you line up for a tin of bad meat and a hard biscuit.

The air in peace is better.

In peace you can let your hair grow, wear yellow, chew gum, forget about making the bed, slouch, quit your job, take a shower alone, hang a shirt up crooked on the hanger, stay out of tanks that shake your insides and give you a headache from the heat.

The hours in peace are shorter.

Peace doesn't make strawberry ice cream cones almost impossible to get.

Peace doesn't make you say your name backward to a lot of strangers who want you to add "Sir!" at the end of every sentence.

You don't have to crawl on your belly under barbed wire in the rain to practise for peace.

Peace doesn't hide a lovely sunset behind a big, ugly mushroom cloud.

If you lose in peace, you can read about it in the next day's newspaper.

The worst thing peace planes do is lose your luggage.

According to most medical reports, peace nerves are not a common ailment, except among Toronto Argo fans.

Peace leaves all the streetlights on so you can get around at night without bumping into buildings or falling down steps you didn't see.

In peace you can pick your friends.

An elderly politician can send a bunch of young people off to peace without their mothers and fathers crying at some train station or airport and wondering if they'll ever see their children again.

There's no embarrassing physical for peace, or age limit.

According to insurance company actuarial tables, people live longer waging total peace.

You can always tell what season it is in peace because peace doesn't burn the leaves off trees or cause the temperature of the neighbourhood suddenly to go up 4,000 degrees.

Peace offensives don't interfere with TV reception.

Peace-ravaged countries have the highest standard of living.

If you send a young person out on peace manoeuvres, about the worst injury he can pick up is a hickey on his neck.

Finally, nobody ever said peace is hell, which is worth remembering.

October 23, 1981

Mrs. Packard was the Iron Lady of my childhood

We've been running stories on bad kids. Kids who don't behave at school. Kids who get in trouble with the law. Kids who go around whacking people and doing damage.

It's too bad Mrs. Packard isn't around to straighten them out.

When I was young, we lived on Tisdale Street in Hamilton. At Number 35. Across the street and two doors up lived Mrs. Packard.

In my lifetime, I've met burly cops, powerful politicians, grumpy athletes, editors who would eat your eye glasses (literally). I once had a neighbour who supplied guns to the mobs.

But nobody scared me like Mrs. Packard. She ruled our block with an iron fist.

When we played ball hockey on the road, which we did all the time, we knew we were doomed if the ball strayed on Mrs. Packard's lawn.

The ball would practically still be in the air when Mrs. Packard would swoop out and grab it.

That would be the end of the game. Even Orville Bell (the biggest kid on the block) and the Stewarts, whose father was a doctor, didn't have enough courage to ask for the ball back.

With Mrs. Packard, there was no appeal. Her look could crumble concrete.

To make things worse, Mrs. Packard's backyard bordered on a school baseball diamond. You could kiss good-bye to any foul tip that went over the fence and landed on her grass.

Mrs. Packard was a two-lawn threat. How she could watch front and back I don't know. But she did.

Asking one of your parents to knock on Mrs. Packard's door for the lost ball was a last resort.

But if you did that, you usually got a bawling out from

your parents who had better things to do than get your ball back. You shouldn't let the ball land on Mrs. Packard's property anyway.

Gloom, gloom.

That was a long time ago, but I have never forgotten Mrs. Packard.

She taught us a lesson.

Respect other people's stuff.

Don't think you are the only person in the world.

Not all people are like your parents.

And, for heaven's sake, shoot straight or the game will be called for lack of a ball.

Give Mrs. Packard some credit. Nobody in our gang— we called ourselves the Tisdale Street Bearcats—wound up in jail, or politics. That's something.

Did I ever tell you about Mrs. Dent who lived next door to Mrs. Packard? She had a Pomeranian dog named Dinky that occasionally got out the door when she wasn't looking.

Mrs. Dent (who had a deep voice) would come out on her porch and yell at us, "Have you seen my Dinky?"

When you're 10, it doesn't get much funnier than that.

Blame Mrs. Packard and Mrs. Dent if you don't like the way I turned out.

I wonder what Mrs. Packard did with all those balls?

March 19, 1990

A child's hopeful leap shows me true meaning of life

I think I have discovered The Meaning of Life.

It's so simple I'm surprised somebody else hasn't discovered it by now.

I would like to say the discovery came to me in a flash or a dream or a bolt of lightning that struck me in the middle of my forehead.

In truth, it happened on the street. On Church Street, of all places.

I was walking along the sidewalk, minding every one else's business, which is what journalists do best, when I noticed a little boy with his mother.

The boy was about three.

Without warning, the little fellow made a jump in the air in an attempt to touch an awning at least 10 feet high.

I broke out laughing.

There was no way on earth he could touch the awning. He might just as well have been reaching for the moon.

But he kept trying.

He made at least three leaps in the air, hand upraised, to reach his impossible goal.

Suddenly I was a little boy, too, and I remembered how many times I had tried to reach a branch, a ledge, a leaf, an awning far, far overhead.

That's when The Meaning of Life hit me — what human beings are all about.

Like that little boy, we are all always trying to reach an awning that tempts us from a distance.

That is what Gorbachev and Bush will attempt this weekend on warships off Malta — to reach their own awning.

Of course, they will fall short, just like the little boy on Church Street.

They will not solve the Cold War, produce peace in every corner of the world, provide hot lunches for the hungry, cure the sick, etc.

But they will try.

The same goes for what is happening in Czechoslovakia, Central America, China, South Africa and other places "round the globe."

There are people of good will everywhere, trying to touch their own personal awnings.

All of us, or most, are trying to write the perfect story, sing the perfect song, find the perfect mate, tell the perfect joke, discover the perfect cure, build the perfect skyscraper, make the perfect car, write the perfect exam, throw the perfect pitch, and live the perfect life.

We will never do it.

Like the little boy on Church Street, we will fall short of the mark. Even Mozart, Da Vinci and Shakespeare wanted to do more.

In life, we do what we can, not what we want. We are intrigued by the impossible, seduced by the untouchable.

That's okay.

Malcolm Muggeridge once said the essence of humour is mortal man striving for immortality.

I think he means as long as little children dream and take running leaps at awnings, human beings will be all right.

It also explains why I walked the rest of the way to work with a smile on my face.

November 29, 1989

To tell the truth, I was spoiled rotten as a kid

I'm glad I'm not a kid today.

I couldn't handle the hours.

When I was young, being a kid was one of the best jobs around.

You'd get up at 8:15 (after your mother wiggled your toes), you'd have breakfast, and then you'd mosey over to school for a 9 o'clock start.

At 4 o'clock you'd knock off for the day.

In the meantime, you had enjoyed two play periods called recesses, and been home from 12 to 1:30 for lunch.

It was a snap and, when I look back, I'm surprised I ever gave up my job as a kid. It had everything, including a five-day week, take-out peanut butter sandwiches and room service if you had a cold.

From what I've observed, kid work has changed a lot from those distant days.

For example, when I walk to work in the morning now, I see loads of kids already on their way to daycare, babysitters and other child centres.

It's hardly dawn and you can spot them — in the backseat of cars, strapped into plastic buddy seats on bicycle fenders, in taxis, in mini-vans.

I don't know what time the average kids get up in Toronto today but if you said 6:30 a.m., I wouldn't be surprised.

Even 5:30 or 6 isn't out of the question if parents have any distance to travel and have to be at office or shop by 8.

And many of today's kids don't get picked up and home again until close to 6 o'clock at night. That's a 12-hour day.

No, ours was the golden age for kids.

Besides the good hours, I never had to carry a house key (which I'd have lost playing street hockey or marbles) to let myself in. Somebody was always home.

I never had to eat lunch with strangers and learn the names of a lot of grown-ups in smocks.

I didn't have to memorize a phone number where my mother or father could be reached if I fell down and got a bleeding nose.

I didn't have to ask permission of a non-family member if I wanted to sprawl on the front veranda with friends and make up nicknames for each other while drinking Freshie and planning where the tent (if we had one) would go in the backyard.

I didn't have to have my name stencilled on all my clothes so a supervisor wouldn't get them mixed up.

Because of the shorter hours and simpler lifestyle, not as much was expected of us either.

When I was a kid my parents didn't expect me to read Tolstoy when I was four, learn a foreign language or play the bassoon when somebody from the office dropped by.

I didn't have to know how to cook my own dinner, get to Winnipeg without help, call the plumber if the toilet backed up or take care of my baby brother by age six.

It was, in short, an undemanding time. I can't remember doing anything worthwhile or practical until I was at least 11 or 12.

Today's kids might think I'm making this up but it's all true. By today's standards, I was spoiled rotten, especially by my mother.

And it was wonderful.

September 24, 1984

Please, can't we all give *that* word a rest?

One of my dreams in life is to go through an entire day without hearing that F word.

The other day I was at the movies and two young men in front of me must have used that F word at least 200 times between them.

They used it as a verb, a noun, an adjective, even as an adverb (something I thought impossible), and as punctuation.

They used it to describe everything from popcorn to a car one apparently admired with passion.

Without that F word, I'd guess their conversation would amount to no more than 25 words, and they talked at least 10 minutes before the movie started.

Now don't think I'm just in for the day from a religious community and have a horse and buggy tied up at the curb.

I have worked as a reporter in hockey dressing rooms. I have laboured in steel mills. I have even spent time in Hamilton, Ontario, and know ministers' sons personally.

But the proliferation of that F word boggles my mind.

It's on T-shirts. It's in movies. It's on TV, especially if you read athletes' lips when they question calls. It's in books. It's on streets with innocent names like Shadeland, Blue Jay Boulevard and Mother Teresa Drive.

Presidents, ingenues in the movies, comics, nursery school kids, Rosedale matrons, morality squad cops, many now use that F word.

Help!

No longer is that F word a shocker. No longer is it a symbol of artistic freedom. No longer is it a unique insult to be heard only a few times in a person's life with stunning effect.

It's become boring, cheap and (to some people) plain disgusting, a sure sign of verbal constipation.

What I'd like is Ottawa's enlistment of Stephen Lewis, our UN ambassador, to come up with some solid substitutes for phrases using that F word.

Lewis has a fulsome vocabulary. Recently, for example, some critics said Lewis wasn't complaining enough about American involvement in Central America.

Replied Lewis: "Fulminating into the void makes little sense."

He also said his UN role "does not permit of orchestrated

spasms of outrage when the outrage is unproductive."

Now that's the kind of mouth we need to come up with alternatives to that F word.

Anyone who can dream up "fulminating into the void" is capable of producing a dozen ways people can show anger, surprise, liberation, what they think of a parking ticket, etc. without resorting to that overworked F word.

A person who deals in "orchestrated spasms" might work wonders with John McEnroe, Eddie Murphy, and the entire roster of the National Hockey League, not to mention the editorial rooms of with-it women's magazines.

If that doesn't work, I'd like the government to declare a 24-hour moratorium on that F word, making it illegal to use that word anywhere in Canada for an entire 24 hours, no matter whom you're trying to impress.

We could appoint F inspectors to prowl the streets, handing out $25 tickets to offenders who break the F word embargo.

Second offenders would have their lips Krazy Glued shut.

March 1, 1985

No one's good for war

According to the Department of National Defence, women are "unsuitable" for combat.

I have news for the Department of National Defence.

So are men.

Men are suitable for selling life insurance, watering the lawn, watching the Blue Jays on TV, playing catch with the kids, driving to the in-laws for Sunday dinner, carrying out the garbage, moving furniture if you want to rearrange the room again, and hugging.

They are not suitable for shooting at, blowing up or

turning into an atomic cinder.

Men are suitable for going fishing when it's still dark, singing semi-bawdy songs around a campfire, looking for a noise in the basement at 3 a.m., holding up a picture for an hour and a half to see if it's straight before you hammer the nail, carrying bags of groceries, throwing a Frisbee, carrying a small person on his shoulders at a Santa Claus parade, understanding a box score, and kissing a knee better.

They are not suitable for clubbing, spearing or spraying with poison gas.

Men are suitable for buying unwanted lingerie, dancing close, putting off plans to wallpaper the kitchen, blushing when a packet of old love letters is discovered, reciting old school yells, reading a book on a snowy night, overdrafting at the bank, wearing a necktie that doesn't go with the suit, losing the sports section, displaying an amazing amount of tolerance for crabgrass, and saying you can't have a gerbil, rat or anything else with a long, skinny tail as a pet.

They are not suitable for impaling, stabbing or throwing hand grenades at.

Men are suitable for storing useless football facts about the Argos, cleaning fish, growing stubble on a holiday weekend, making up excuses why it's not a good time to clean up the basement, teaching a small person how to ride a two-wheeler, getting a hot dog or pretzel with mustard at a sports event, answering the phone for a daughter and fibbing she is out, making simple meals, walking in the rain, and telling dreams to.

They are not suitable for bombing, torpedoing or frying with napalm.

Men are suitable for writing dumb poetry, building things, holding hands with when there are a million stars in the sky, talking to in front of a fire, looking inside the hood of a car that won't start and not having a clue what he's looking at, producing a Visa card for a daughter's first pair of long pants, complaining about the weather, growing a moustache, drying dishes, finding a nice restaurant, working at a job that isn't all that exciting, and scratching your back.

They are not suitable for germ, nuclear or outer space warfare.

Men are suitable for starting the barbecue, gathering wood at a beach weenie roast, whispering awful lies in an ear, sending to a supermarket for a few things (provided you give him a note and list the items aisle-by-aisle), hanging around the water fountain, impolitely whistling at females, letting out the cat, writing post-dated cheques for the mortgage, and cuddling up to on a cold night.

They are not suitable for wounding, hurting or killing.

When departments of national defence all over the world realize both men and women are "unsuitable" for combat, we'll all be better off.

May 24, 1985

Listen up, grads, it's time for some real education

May is graduation month, a time when young people go forth to face Life. While they are brilliant about the French Revolution and squares on the hypotenuses of triangles, some may be a little weak on practical knowledge.

For them I have prepared this— *Words to Live By.*

The superintendent in your new apartment is not like your parents, especially when it comes to paying the rent.

Unless you are over 60 years of age or have a million dollars in T-bills, it isn't a plus to be referred to at the office as a "real character."

Buy the expensive toilet paper. It's worth the difference.

Never go on a blind date with a person described as a "lot of fun" or having a "nice personality."

Neighbours are not impressed if you use a flag as a curtain once you are over the age of 23.

You'll never learn anything worthwhile in a letter addressed, "Dear Householder . . ."

"Easy payments" aren't.

Jealousy in a boyfriend is a lot more attractive than jealousy in a husband.

Avoid at all cost friends who casually mention they have a kitten to give away.

Don't be disappointed you can't live nearly as well now you have a job as you did when you were at university and without income. That is how life works.

The bill to fix a car is never under $200.

Universities keep in touch with grads they didn't think would amount to anything by asking for donations to help educate students they don't think will amount to anything.

Resist offers to go out for a "quick one" after work. The only people to get rich from the traditional "quick one" after work are the Bronfmans and Molsons.

Eating something green every day doesn't mean jujubes, chocolate mint ice cream cones or a piece of bacon that's been left in the refrigerator too long.

The first person you'll meet after graduation will be an insurance salesman. Do not judge your personality and charm by the way he laughs at your jokes or compliments your taste in clothes.

Make your bed every morning. It's good discipline. It also puts off their guard any members of the opposite sex you've coaxed back to your apartment.

The giant size carton of cottage cheese is never a bargain.

The world is filled with restaurants with plants hanging from the ceiling and waiters named Randy wanting to sell you $6 drinks with cute names and paper umbrellas stuck in fruit slices. Avoid them.

Also stay away from loan companies, plastic shoes, companions who need $20 till payday and long discussions at the office cooler over last night's episode of the "A Team."

If your soul cries out for at least one luxury in life, start with a good bath towel.

A Big Mac does not constitute gourmet eating in the grownup world.

Never sit in anything in a car showroom you can't afford.

There are two ways to disguise a bad meal: candlelight and ketchup.

Marrying the boss's child is getting a promotion the hard way. Take night courses instead. At least your weekends are free.

A living room decorated with Humphrey Bogart posters gets boring.

Learning to iron a shirt is more valuable than being able to rattle off the names of the Fathers of Confederation.

Don't leave dishes in the sink. They attract germ-carrying bugs and scare off cheque-bearing parents.

Don't waste time. The next 50 years go faster than you think.

April 30, 1986

We can be thankful for so many things

This is Thanksgiving, so it only seems proper to list some of the things I'm thankful for.

I'm thankful for the vast fields of prairie wheat that feed us and the world.

I'm thankful for scooped necklines.

I'm thankful for the wonderful advances made by medical researchers who work tirelessly against disease.

I'm thankful for Tony Fernandez, who can go to his right or left and make the Big Play.

I'm thankful for fish in our seas, minerals in our ground, trees in our forests, and French vanilla in our ice cream stands.

I'm thankful for our VCR, which allows me to tape David Letterman and watch it at a decent hour.

I'm thankful for autumn leaves that bring beauty into our lives and serenity to our souls, although they do take a lot of raking.

I'm thankful for iced tea, which I think should be available year-round in restaurants and not just in the summer.

I'm thankful for the little birds that cheer our days, provided they don't cheer all over the car. I'm thankful for long-legged women who, at great personal risk, wear skirts with slits at the sides even when the weather turns nasty.

I'm thankful for our great north, which constantly reminds us of the power and grace of nature, and where the good hockey players come from.

I'm thankful for granola, field berries yogurt and red Delicious apples.

I'm thankful for billowy clouds that give me something to stare at, and fill me with wonder . . . about whether I should take my raincoat.

I'm thankful for the Three Stooges, especially Larry.

I'm thankful for those who have gone before me so I could inherit wonderful books, marvellous works of art, and breathtaking cities like Rome, Vienna, Paris and Medicine Hat.

I'm thankful for red jujubes.

I'm thankful for inventors who solved great mysteries so I can survive cold winters, fly through the sky, flick a switch to banish the darkness, talk to loved ones thousands of miles away, and watch "Cheers" on TV.

I'm thankful for mashed potatoes (not the instant kind), with gravy.

I'm thankful for the Laurentians where I spend summer days on a raft and wouldn't trade places with anybody in the world, including Wayne Gretzky.

I'm thankful for Kathleen Turner, Kim Basinger and the person who designed the bathing suit worn by the female lead in *Crocodile Dundee*.

I'm thankful for a generous family that lets me use the bathroom in our house at least once a day, twice if I'm quick about it.

I'm thankful for the person who invented words, especially *hug*, which is my favourite and easy to spell.

I'm thankful for money of which I don't have a lot but enough to get by, provided my wife doesn't go crazy when she gets the new chesterfield for the front room.

I'm thankful for the discoverer of sleep.

I'm thankful for dogs, the finest four-legged companion a person can have, provided the kids will feed them and walk them twice a day, which they never do, especially if it's raining.

I'm thankful for all the seasons of the year that make Canada interesting, but I'm a little less thankful for March, ugh.

I'm thankful for the Royal Canadian Air Farce, Bob McClure, Karen Kain, Second City, Tony Manis (my dentist), P. Trudeau, Max Ward, Wendell Clark (if he'd stop fighting so much), and every other Canadian except the one who swiped my kid's bike.

Finally, I'm thankful for you without whose daily 25 cents I'd have to find a job.

October 13, 1986

I could never kill another living thing

I'm a lily-livered, bleeding heart, yellow-bellied sissy when it comes to capital punishment.

I couldn't pull the switch on a fellow human being.

It is not that I'm some kind of saint, but there is something deep inside that would doom me to a thousand sleepless nights if I played God with someone else's life.

Why, I even get annoyed when somebody senselessly strips leaves from a tree branch or steps on a flower or holds a frog to see it squirm.

Maybe it's because I am growing older and have more respect for life.

Last year, for example, one of our house plants was left out in the direct sunlight by accident. By the time we discovered the mistake, the poor thing was broiled to little more than a twig.

I guess the smart thing would have been to ditch it.

But I wanted to give it a chance. Life, as I say, gets more precious the more you see of it.

The plant didn't show much sign of anything for weeks, but finally a little new green began to sprout at the tip of the main stem. The urge to live is that strong.

The plant has a few sprouts this summer but still looks scruffy and odd. No matter. It's my favourite plant and (I confess) I sometimes say things like, "Way to go, plant!" I'm rooting for it.

In print, this sounds pretty dumb, but I have this reverence for life. Don't ask me how it got there. I have seen people die and know how hard they struggled to live.

I guess I worship life. It is my religion.

Don't get me wrong. I know there are evil people and good people with evil thoughts. I know about awful crimes. I have been a police reporter and seen my share of mutilated bodies.

But I have never seen anything that would cause me to place a hangman's noose around another human being's neck.

Put them in a cell and throw away the key? Yes.

Deprive them of freedom and dignity and privacy forever? Yes. Make them work for their keep? Certainly.

But kill them to teach them killing is wrong? No. I could not. Therefore, I do not want the state to do for me what I would not do myself.

If one victim of a horrible murder could be brought back to life by killing his or her murderer, I would make that bargain. If one child victim could be made whole again, I would help build the scaffold.

But it doesn't work that way.

Killing some madman, some doped-up killer, some passion-plagued lover, some moronic hired gun, none of that will create one spark of life or undo the past.

Do we ask the death sentence for some industrialist whose products spill death into our air and water? Do we ask death for a clever business operator who can close down a factory and put hundreds out of work while making a lovely profit for himself?

Do we ask death for generals in braided hats who sit in posh offices and daily plan the destruction of half of this earth's people with their missiles? Do we dangle a rope under the nose of politicians who lie and sell off our land?

No, but some kid with only three brain cells working who goes nuts in the street, and can't afford a fancy lawyer, well, we talk about hanging him.

I don't know what I would do if trapped in an alley with a maniac and it was his life or mine. I would fight to the end, I suppose.

But I do not think I was put on this earth to kill people if there is any other choice.

April 29, 1987

Silence much sweeter than noisy candy

I have one nephew. His name is Mark Lautens—Dr. Mark Lautens to be fancy. He is 28 years old and a professor at the University of Toronto.

Of course we're proud of him. And it is very nice to have a professor walk into the house and say, "Hello, Uncle Gary."

But enough advertisement.

I have a challenge for Mark.

Mark joined the U of T staff this summer after finishing two years of post-doctoral work at Harvard. His field is chemistry, something I have trouble spelling, let alone doing.

With all his education in science, I'd like Mark to produce something that has eluded mankind for billions and billions of years, something that has baffled the best minds, something even more complicated than talking dashboards and one-size pantyhose.

I talk of non-crinkly candy wrappers.

As readers of these scribbles know, I am a movie addict. Movies are my entertainment, my therapy, my escape, my hobby—well, put me in a darkened room with Barbra Streisand, Sean Connery, Steve Martin and the like, and I am a happy man.

Only one thing detracts from my joy—crinkly candy wrappers.

I can handle popcorn munchers. I can overlook soft-drink slurpers. I don't even kidney-punch talkers if they keep it down.

But I draw the line at crinkly candy wrappers.

How many times have I been engrossed in a suspense scene only to have someone in the next row tear open a piece of foil, rattle a sheet of plastic, shake a cardboard box or unwrap a guaranteed moisture-proof bit of wax paper. Probably 57 million.

It is as offensive to the serious movie-goer's ear as the brakes of a garbage truck on a wet morning.

One of the worst offenders is the thoughtful candy user who insists on unwrapping that mint or cough drop from purse or pocket in very slow stages, as if doing it slowly reduces the decibel level.

Apparently they think removing a tooth with a series of little tugs reduces the pain too.

I know—I'm a theatre crank. I probably don't like people coming along the row behind and knocking my head either. I probably even object when somebody's feet rest on the back of my seat or a fellow patron wants to talk to the screen or wolf-whistle at the sensitive love scene.

No, I can semi-soldier through that. Even sticky floors and half-filled tubs of popcorn left in the dark to kick over don't totally leave me frothing at the gums.

It's crinkly candy wrappers I'd like nephew Mark to remove from the face of the earth for starters.

He can forget about playing in Japanese seaweed, synthesizing toe jam, looking at wriggly things under his microscope, probing the mysteries of stomach gas, or whatever it is he does in the lab.

Do us all a favour and tackle the big problem—making noiseless candy wrappers.

If he pulls it off, he could be looking at a Nobel prize or at least the Famous Players man-of-the-year award.

December 7, 1987

Wishy-washy agnostics leave me feeling good

Every now and then I feel the urge to get down on my knees and thank God for the agnostics.

Some dismiss them as people who can't make up their minds about religion. Ask if there's an Almighty and the best an agnostic can come up with is, "Beats me."

They are just as shaky about heaven, an afterlife, reincarnation or celestial choirs. They say they just don't know.

Okay, they may be spiritually wishy-washy.

But look at the positive side of agnostics.

They don't come to your front door Sunday morning with pamphlets. They don't build expensive theme parks. They don't operate banks, mail order houses or cosmetics companies as a sideline.

They don't go on TV and say they will drop dead if you don't send them $20 million by the end of the month.

They don't offer cash prizes for killing authors they don't like.

They don't hang around airports or in front of the Eaton Centre begging money to further agnostic projects.

They don't brainwash children who then have to be deprogrammed.

They don't throw rocks, booby-trap cars, fire plastic bullets, put bombs on jets, hold innocent people hostage or assassinate prime ministers on the excuse they are acting on instructions from a higher power.

They don't get all blubbery and blame the Devil if they get caught in a motel with a perfumed hussy.

They seldom appear as a group on the 10 o'clock news shouting slogans, waving placards, going limp when the police arrive or burning someone who disagrees with them in effigy.

They don't have a list of banned books.

They don't sell raffle tickets on expensive cars to support their lack of faith. They don't ask for special meals on planes, at athletic banquets or wedding receptions. They don't have a box number where you're invited to send pledges.

Females and males pretty well have equal status in agnosticism. They don't lobby politicians, chop off hands or claim an exclusive pipeline to Truth, Wisdom and Virtue.

They don't feel insulted every time someone opens his mouth. They make no threats about fire and brimstone. They have no policy about veils, hats, incense, eye make-up or dancing close. They don't hold potluck dinners.

Mind you, agnostics don't have a clue why they are on this earth. They don't know who to thank if they win the World Series or Oscar.

They aren't sure who made the tree.

They have no songbook and only a few secular holidays. They have no side to root for in Ireland, the Middle East, Asia or Sunday morning on TV. They have no souvenirs.

Still, in a world in which every religion claims to have the answer, surely there's room for a group that claims to have no answer at all.

God bless them, I say.

And amen.

February 24, 1989

Some simple rules to help people in news tell right from wrong

People seem to have trouble these days telling right from wrong. Well-educated politicians, heads of charities, famous athletes and even religious leaders are on Page 1 because they can't tell the difference.

Here are some simple rules for them:

It's wrong to take things that don't belong to you.

It's wrong to make promises you don't keep.

It's wrong to play rough and hurt people.

It's wrong to act differently just because nobody is looking.

It's wrong to say one thing and do another.

It's wrong to always want your way.

It's wrong not to share.

It's wrong to cheat and take an unfair advantage.

It's wrong to play the radio loud.

It's wrong to give away something that isn't yours.

When people trust you, it's wrong to let them down.

It's wrong to use swear words and tell dirty stories.

It's wrong to make fun of people for things they can't help.

It's wrong to try to run other people's lives until yours is perfect.

Laughing is really important. So are good manners.

It's wrong to ignore those who are less fortunate.

It's wrong not to do your best.

It's wrong to lie.

It's wrong to want something so badly you'll do anything to get it.

It's wrong to envy someone who has achieved something special through hard work and dedication.

Dreams are better to chase than money.

It's wrong to think you're the only one in the world.

It's wrong to have eyes bigger than your belly.

It's wrong to stay up late on school nights.

It's wrong to boast about yourself and toot your own horn.

Hitting is wrong.

It's wrong to race around not looking where you're going.

It's wrong to waste a day.

It's wrong not to have time for people, or to smell the flowers.

It's wrong not to tell people you care.

It's wrong not to answer letters.

It's wrong to be late for dinner unless you call home first.

It's wrong to pretend to be something you're not.

It's wrong to make people afraid.

It's wrong to talk and eat at the same time.

It's wrong to talk without thinking.

It's wrong to go through a day without doing some good.

It's wrong not to try.

It's wrong to throw sand, or dirt.

It's wrong to judge anything only on whether or not you'll be caught.

It's wrong not to have a passion for life and all living things.

Those are some simple rules my mother taught me many years ago. She had no PhD. She only attended Maple Leaf School in Morden, Manitoba.

But apparently she was wiser than many people who get their names on Page 1 these days.

June 16, 1989

Dirty planet needs
a slick lobbyist

The environment is the Number 1 problem of the decade but nobody seems to be doing much about it.

The reason is obvious. There are no kickbacks, pay-offs or exorbitant profits to be made in the environment industry.

Companies that produce arms are willing to make enormous contributions to a politician's campaign because they know they can sell a bomber back to the government for half a billion dollars.

Even a screw can be palmed off for $45 if it's in a jet that goes twice the speed of sound and can blow up a country in a split second.

But what can you get for a clean beach? Practically nothing.

Nobody is willing to slip a politician a nice cheque for a lovely view or a tree that isn't being eaten by acid rain.

There is just no profit in clean air.

Ask yourself this: When was the last time you heard of a central American dictator going into the clean air business and shipping pollution-free oxygen to North America in containers marked "musical instruments"?

Or when did you read a newspaper report about a billionaire wanting to take over waterfront property so he could leave it free of condos, business blocks and highrise tourist attractions?

And if there was an item in the business section about a Toronto law firm getting involved in a mega-merger so it can better defend the rights of water birds to enjoy garbage-free nesting areas, I must have missed it.

If we want to clean up the environment, obviously we have to find some way to make it profitable for politicians, tycoons and other Big Cheeses who, up till now, can only make a killing ruining the environment, not saving it.

Personally, I'm convinced politicians would rezone a dirty factory into parkland or side with the sea lions and seals over the big oil companies—provided they can still run expensive election campaigns, go on junkets to Hawaii, and find lucrative jobs as consultants when their public days are over.

Can nature guarantee that?

We know the answer.

Elephants, maple trees, rivers and all that stuff don't have a dime. They couldn't buy a dinner at Winston's or even a TTC token among them.

What we need is somebody like Mother West Wind or Jimmy Skunk or Farmer Brown's meadow to inherit a pile of money and start spreading it around, hiring a good lobbyist with government connections, taking a few well-placed media types out for drinks, buying tickets to politicians' dinners.

Well, you know the sort of thing.

That would at least provide the level playing field politicians are always talking about when they discuss money.

Maybe then we'll start to get serious about cleaning up this planet we share.

But until Bambi and the Laughing Brook and the Purple Hills (where the Merry Little Breezes go at night) have as big a line of credit at the bank as Exxon, Boeing and GM, well, it won't be much of a fight.

October 23, 1989

You, too, can wreck your life and be a total loser

How to be a loser.

Feel sorry for yourself.

Blame others when things go wrong.

Blame your parents, the system, your teachers, your name, society—anyone.

Never point a finger at yourself.

When people say Beethoven wrote great music when he was deaf, or Stephen Hawking has great thoughts even though he can't feed himself, reply, "That's different."

Never let an excuse go unused.

Don't try.

Quit as soon as the going gets a little tough.

Settle for second best.

Claim everyone who gets ahead is "crooked."

Regard going to school and working hard as something for suckers.

Be jealous of those who are successful because of education and hard work.

Turn bitter. Turn mean.

Find some sleaze and make him or her your best friend. Together, look down on everyone else.

Show society you aren't going to play life by its rules.

Whine when society leaves you behind.

Waste time. Treat your body like a garbage pail. Ruin your brain.

Reject a helping hand.

Do anything or say anything to stay in with a gang. Don't ever say, "No," to a stupid suggestion for fear you'll look like a sissy.

Pick some witless celebrity as a role model, someone who thinks it's smart to talk about violence, dope and thumbing your nose at old values.

Be a follower.

Never even try to learn a skill society can use.

Look for a get-rich quick scheme. Never falter from the conviction there is a shortcut to the top and that you'll be the first person in history to find it.

Don't stick at anything.

Treat youth as if it will go on forever. Don't think about the future.

Make a lot of noise but never say anything worth remembering.

Think of yourself as the first person ever to have a hard time, ever to have an uphill climb, ever to face a challenge that scares you. Think of yourself as "Poor me."

Listen to the angry, the vicious, and choose them as your leaders.

Don't try to understand anyone else. Consider it their problem to understand you.

If you've got problems, make them worse by screwing up more.

Don't look at what you have going for you in life and build on that. Concentrate on what you don't have and get discouraged.

Don't get smart, get even.

Take it for granted parents are always wrong and 100 percent against you.

If you have a rotten home life, let it destroy you. Let it ruin the next 75 years of life, too, just to show your parents what they did to you.

Carry a grudge.

Expect perfection — in others.

Don't try to control your temper. Let it explode if it wants.

Hang around places where trouble hangs out.

Don't think of consequences. Don't think of responsibilities. Don't think.

Be last to leave every party.

Never understand there are chances and opportunities in your life that are envied by even the mighty.

Believe in nothing. Or no one.

By following these simple rules, I guarantee anyone can be a loser.

June 18, 1990

What kind of person would try to kill a sparrow?

This is a silly little story.

It involves no dictators, no armies, no pronouncements from some world capital.

It involves a bird.

A tiny bird. A bird with no fancy credentials. A street bird.

A sparrow.

But this bird has been in my mind for several days. I have talked about it over the dinner table. I have discussed it with friends who may have been bored.

This is the story.

At the end of our street is a park. At one time it was a service station, so you understand it isn't quite as grand as Kensington Gardens in London or Paris' Jardin des Tuileries.

But it is green space where office workers can take their lunch and joggers can take their pulses.

A few days ago my wife was walking through the park around suppertime.

It was last Friday and no one was in the park.

But she heard a noise.

She looked around and there, on the ground, was a frantic sparrow.

It was locked in a plastic bag with half a sandwich.

Apparently someone had coaxed the sparrow into the

bag with the sandwich — and then zip-locked the bag shut.

Whoever did it then walked away, leaving the frightened bird inside.

Of course, my wife unlocked the bag and the sparrow happily flew away.

End of story.

I told you it wasn't much. I don't think it would make a newscast or even offer a photo op for an eager politician.

It's just a story about cruelty to a bird.

Believe me, I am not a victim of too many Thornton Burgess stories read to me at childhood. Nor do I have a strange sense of values.

I know there are wars going on, children being killed, diseases ravaging dear friends, catastrophes levelling villages.

I know.

But I couldn't help wondering what kind of person would deliberately lure a little bird into a bag — and then leave it trapped to suffocate.

How could anyone do it? Why would anyone do it?

Was it a prank? A sick mind? A thoughtless gesture?

I have no answer.

It's sad to think of someone getting amusement out of tormenting a little scrap of life only looking for a bit of crust.

Heaven knows there's enough hurting going on in the world today without adding to it.

If I've learned anything in life (and there may be some argument about that), it's that you get more pleasure from giving pleasure than giving pain.

Making people happy makes you happy. That goes for little birds, too.

Happiness is like a boomerang. You can't get rid of it. You throw it at someone, and it comes right back to you.

Hold a door. Kiss a bruise. Hug a grandma. Fix a

problem. Help a stranger.

You get a smile right back. And it makes you feel good.

I don't know what you get from trapping a sparrow in a plastic bag.

Not as much as throwing it a few crumbs.

August 20, 1990

Call it corny, but there's still such a thing as trust

I am a big city columnist.

I have seen everything. Been everywhere.

Yawn.

I am as classy as all git out.

But over the holiday I was shocked. Stunned. If I didn't have witnesses, I'd swear I was the victim of a hallucination. That my peepers were playing tricks.

Listen to this.

We decided to go hiking at Rattlesnake Point. When the kids were young, we did it often.

I couldn't count the times Jackie yelled at little Richard, "Don't lean so far over the cliff." Or, "Don't pick that up."

It was a lot of fun.

So Rattlesnake Point has a lot of memories for us and we still go back once or twice a year.

To get to Rattlesnake you have to go to Burlington and make a right turn on the Appleby Line.

We were only a mile or two from the park when the bizarre episode took place.

On the corner of a lane leading to a distant farmhouse was a roadstand piled high with corn.

No one was tending the stand.

All that was there was a sign:
"Fresh Corn
$3 a dozen
Please leave money
Please be honest."
That was it.

The farmer was leaving it to the customer to serve him or herself. The farmer was counting on the customer to be honest.

Being a big city columnist, of course, I suspected a trick.

My list of possibilities included the following:

- exploding corn,
- hidden trap door in front of corn stand,
- TV camera shooting for "America's Funniest Home Videos,"
- vicious dog hiding behind cash box on counter just waiting to get its teeth on a juicy leg.

My wife ignored my warnings and said she wanted a dozen corn from the stand. "Have you any money?" she asked.

I said I had a $5 bill.

"I'll make change," she replied.

"You can't make change for yourself," I said. "Does Loblaws let you play in their till? Could you count out Eaton's money?"

My wife paid no attention at all, filled up a bag (on the counter) with corn, opened up the cash box, put in the $5 bill—and took out two loonies.

You could have driven a Buick down my mouth. It was open that far.

That is the story.

It is 1990. People are yelling at each other on the front page of the newspaper every day. They are calling each other liars, Hitlers, old hags, traitors.

And on the Appleby Line (near Rattlesnake Point) a

farmer has a corn stand where strangers pick their corn, pay for it—and make their own change.

What we are talking about is trust.

Honesty.

Faith in our fellow human beings.

Sweet innocence.

Oh, how I wish it would catch on.

Don't you?

September 5, 1990

We can afford to wage war— but not to save lives

Do you think mankind will ever smarten up? Are we just too stupid to survive?

Please forgive my sour mood.

But I have lost another friend to cancer—Mike Walton. He was a bright, decent man. A family guy with two nice kids.

And he's dead at 44.

What a waste. What a loss.

Cancer is our real foe. And heart disease. And MS. And AIDS. And strokes. And . . .

But we spend billions on dumb wars.

Does George Bush go on TV and call on his people to fight cancer? Does Saddam Hussein blast cancer with every nasty name he can put his tongue to? Do Gorbachev, Mulroney, Major, Shamir and all the other big players vow to put an end to cancer?

No.

They call each other names and say death to the enemy.

But they have the enemy wrong.

It's not some scared civilian in Baghdad. It's not some college kid in Miami. It's not some baby in Tel Aviv. It's not some working man in Lithuania, Pretoria or Tibet.

It's disease. It's hunger. It's bad water. It's foul air. It's cancer.

We can spend a billion dollars a day to fight a useless war. We can build warplanes at $15 million a pop. We can mass-produce $1 million missiles. We can sail aircraft carriers that cost $500,000 a day to operate.

No sweat.

But we can't pay nurses a decent wage. We can't keep open hospital wards. We can't find money for research. We can't finance medical schools properly.

Are we nuts?

The United States, the wealthiest country in the world, can't afford a national health plan.

But it will blow billions just to grab a tyrant like Noriega and toss him in a cell.

It will throw away billions to show some tinpot egomaniac who is boss in the Middle East.

Meanwhile, young men like Mike Walton die of cancer.

Forgive me if I have this passion about cancer. Like everyone, I have lost too many friends to that awful curse.

A few months ago my old pal Bob Pennington at the *Sun* died of cancer. Not long ago Yvonne Seon of this newspaper died of cancer. She was 40, mother of a young child.

My mother died of cancer at 65. My father died of cancer at 78.

The list goes on.

Maybe money wouldn't produce a cure for all the cancers. Maybe all the varieties of cancer are too baffling for the human mind to solve. Maybe it's a stone wall too high for our talents to climb.

I don't know.

But I get tired of watching lovely people suffer these terrible deaths.

I get tired of world leaders always saying they can't afford schools, they can't afford sanitation, they can't afford decent food.

But they always seem able to find money for the latest bomber, the shiniest submarine, the newest death gas.

The national debt means nothing—not if it's for war. We empty our pockets, tie yellow ribbons to trees and cheer the death rattle.

What a mad sense of values.

My religion is life.

Too bad this world is so intent on wasting its treasure on death.

February 6, 1991

Police critics should walk a beat in officers' shoes

Premier Bob, Susan Eng and just about every other politician in town have a lot to say about the police.

Fair enough.

We all want the best police possible—and none of that goon stuff we've seen on TV from Los Angeles.

But I do have one suggestion.

Before making any more speeches about the police, I think Premier Bob, Susan Eng and the others should:

Go out on street patrol at 3 a.m. with the cops and, maybe, even check a few dark alleys.

Break up a fight or two in a bar.

Work the traffic detail after a major event.

Investigate a homicide, search the body for clues, talk to

the witnesses, look into the victim's life, etc.

Make a bust with the drug squad on a crack house.

Roll on the ground with a person whacked out on booze, chemicals or a mental problem.

Talk to a woman who has been raped.

Pry a victim of a drunk driver out of a car.

Try to talk sense to someone barricaded in a building, someone with an automatic gun and a hostage.

Hold back a crowd at a wild demonstration where there's pushing, shoving, name-calling and an occasional flying rock.

Spend a day or two in the cells with someone who has murdered a child, just to see what makes them tick.

Talk to the families of cops. Discuss the stress, the shifts, the media.

Sit in court occasionally and listen to evidence.

Step into the middle of a domestic disturbance with people who have lost control of their tempers and are at the point of reaching for a butcher knife.

Sit in a cruiser chasing bank robbers through city streets at wild speeds.

Investigate a few housebreakings where vandals have destroyed personal belongings for no reason and scribbled obscene words on the walls.

Do first aid on the loser in a knife fight at a dance hall.

Listen to abuse from a motorist who doesn't feel he should get a ticket for cutting in and out on the Gardiner.

Organize a search for a missing child last seen with a stranger in a schoolyard.

Write out a report for an elderly person bilked of life savings by a sweet-talking con man.

Try reasoning with someone swinging a bat.

Break up a noisy party at 2 a.m. and tell 20 or 30 rowdy people to keep it down because neighbours are complaining.

Duck a bullet or two.

Watch someone you've nailed on a sex offence get let off because some smart lawyer says the case was too long going to trial.

Okay, that's the list.

I'm not saying Premier Bob, Susan Eng and the others aren't right, or that they shouldn't give an opinion.

I just think theory improves with a good dose of reality.

April 12, 1991

Memo to the do-gooders: give taxpayers a break

Memo:

To politicians, social workers, editorial writers, activists and other people with big ideas.

We are running as fast as we can.

Canadian taxpayers, I mean.

We are trying our best. We are working our hardest. We are going flat out.

So stop giving us a hard time.

Stop thinking up new ways to spend our money.

We have causes coming out our ears.

We know hospitals need more money. We know education needs more money. We know more money is needed for medical research. We know our army is pinched for funds. We know Indians, single mothers, AIDS victims, young people, university students and refugee claimants want more.

But give us a break.

We are carrying as big a load as we can.

Do you realize how difficult it is to raise a family, clothe the kids, buy any kind of home, put away a little something for old age?

Do you realize we're taxed to death now?

So stop always demanding more.

We're trying to clean up dirty air and murky water. We're trying to find a place to put the garbage. We're trying to take care of pensioners, the sick, the unemployed, the disadvantaged.

Believe me, we're trying.

We've got a huge national debt. The job picture in the Atlantic provinces is grim. Farmers say they are just hanging on. Workers need retraining. Companies say they need a hand to survive. Brian wants more senators on the payroll.

We know.

We know far-off countries want aid, that the U.N. wants our cheque, that the north needs a break, that Hibernia will take a major investment, that an icebreaker for the Arctic would come in handy, that every kid should have a good lunch, that the drug fight needs more support, that the courts are overcrowded, that the police are short-staffed, that public transit requires new equipment, that factories will have to spruce up to compete with the Japanese, that low-cost housing is wonderful.

We know.

Why do you think we're puffing? Why do you think we're weary? We can't tap-dance any faster.

You spout off and tell us what is wrong and how much money it will take to fix it.

And then you look at us.

You put out your hand. You say you are stunned by what you see. You write that we are falling behind.

Well, cool it.

We are not blind.

We can see for ourselves that the roads are overcrowded. We want to save the whales, restock the oceans, preserve the forests, make the waterfront safe for swimming.

We want an Olympic team with the best of training facilities. We want free education all the way for everyone. We want a cure for cancer, higher minimum wages and a car in every garage. We aren't anti-opera house.

But we can only do so much.

All you do is ask, complain, point in indignation, berate, scold.

We're tired of it.

We can't solve all the world's problems. We can't carry the burdens of billions of people. We can't feed everyone on the globe or send them all medicine.

We are doing our very best.

So cut out the lectures. Declare a moratorium for six months. Give your finger a rest and stop pointing at us.

We are only human.

(signed) The poor benighted Canadian taxpayer

October 1, 1990

4

That Man/Woman Thing

Women are flat stubborn over high heels

One of the special moments in a man's life is when the woman of his dreams finally surrenders and agrees to slip into something uncomfortable. That can mean only two things: high heels.

Men love women in high heels. It is a fact of life. And the higher and spikier the heel the better.

Alas, it is also a fact of life that women hate high heels as much as men love them. That is probably the major difference between the sexes.

Frankly, I can't blame the stronger sex (females) for preferring loafers, deck shoes, Adidas, moccasins, saddle shoes—anything with a flat heel. It can't be easy teetering around on a heel the size of a dime and at an altitude requiring clearance from Pearson International to make a turn.

In my own personal cave, you can't believe the struggle I go through to get The Light Of My Life into high heels.

Before Jackie will move so much as a single tootsie out of her Wallabees into anything with a high heel, I have to fill out a questionnaire:

1. Are we walking?

2. If we take the car, are you going to park in a real lot next to where we are going or are you going to look for a free spot on the street about eight blocks from our destination?

3. Are we going to have to stand up during the evening?

4. After we've been where we're going, are you going to say, "Let's go for a little walk," instead of getting right in the car and heading home?

5. What's wrong with wearing comfortable shoes

where we're going and changing into high heels at the last minute?

6. Am I going to have to walk across somebody's soft lawn in the dark?

7. Are you positively sure we aren't walking?

8. Are there steps where we're going?

9. Do you know for sure there's broadloom on the floor and not just-waxed hardwood or are you only guessing about that part?

10. If there's a buffet, will you bring food to me on the chesterfield?

Only if I answer the quiz to my wife's complete satisfaction will she put on high heels, especially the red ones with the little straps that never stay up.

I'm not sure how many pairs of high heels my wife's collected over the years (perhaps five or six) but at a guess I'd say the total mileage on them would be about 15 yards, 20 tops, and that's counting distance covered when trying them on in the shoe store.

You can practically see yourself in the soles of her high heel shoes, they're that shiny. No wonder. If you eliminate time spent on elevators, they've hardly moved.

To be 100 percent truthful, there isn't much good to say about high heels. They must be murder on the wearer's legs, not to mention spinal column. They get caught in grates. To drive a car in them can't be a treat. And I've personally watched them sink into the asphalt on a hot day.

Still, men everywhere are thrilled high heels have made a fashion comeback and are even acceptable with jeans, shorts or short skirts.

I just want to tell women that men everywhere appreciate the sacrifice.

October 23, 1985

Heavenly bliss? Umm, no thanks, Pope John Paul

Pope John Paul had some good news and some bad news for us at his most recent general audience.

The good news is that men and women retain their identities in heaven. The bad news is that there is no sex in heaven.

How the revelation hit you, I don't know, but I suspect a lot of people spent the weekend hugging and kissing, trying to get in as much sex as possible before the drought sets in.

If a squirrel is smart enough to store nuts for bleak times ahead, we'd be pretty dumb if we didn't try to get in a supply of naughty-naughty to tide us over Eternity.

But I wonder.

As far as I can figure out, the only group not put in a sour mood by the Vatican announcement were the world's cartoonists. In the weeks ahead they'll undoubtedly make a lot of money on the theme of a sexless heaven inhabited by men and women.

That got me thinking. Why should I, just because I can't draw be left out of this little bonanza? Herewith then are a few of my own cartoons, please use your imagination to fill in the drawing lines.

First cartoon: We have two men watching a bevy of Bo Derek look-alikes as they cavort in a lush pool that has a sign posted on the wall, "No sex, please, we're angels." The one fellow has a sad expression and is saying, "This isn't my idea of heaven."

Second cartoon: A couple of men are leaning on the Pearly Gates. They are looking down from a cloud at a party in progress in another part of heaven. The cloud they are looking at is labelled, "Muslims only." Says one of the men,

"They had oil when they were living, and now they've got sex. Talk about getting the best of both worlds."

Third cartoon: It's Saturday night. A middle-aged couple who arrived in heaven that very day are getting ready for bed. There is a glint in his eye. She: "Oh, Harold, not tonight. I've got a headache." He: "So what else is new."

Fourth cartoon: A man who obviously was a company president in life is putting on his best dress wings and grumbling at his wife. Says he in the caption, "Another evening of bloody harp music, I suppose."

Fifth cartoon: A man is walking down the main street in heaven. It is the legendary Casanova. Two women, one of them his landlady, are observing from windows of the building he has just left. Says the landlady: "You wouldn't believe the cold water bill he ran up last month."

Sixth cartoon: A husband and wife watch as their incredibly gorgeous daughter in a provocative mini skirt gets inside her date's wildly decorated van parked at the curb. The relaxed father beams and says, "Boy, this is heaven!"

Seventh cartoon: Two snakes are coiled on chairs behind a roadside stand in heaven. Apples are stacked on the counter. "Eight million, four hundred and twenty-seven thousand years and still no sale," one partner bitterly comments to the other. "Maybe we should try pears."

Eighth cartoon: Two women are looking at a Robert Redford-type as he leans over a water fountain in heaven. Whispers one: "I understand he intellectualizes on first dates."

And finally . . .

Ninth cartoon: A rabbi and a United Church minister are walking down the street in heaven and the one says to the other, "I still think he was crazy to trade sex for bingo."

December 7, 1981

105

Nothing smelly or sexy for Christmas, if you please

At this time of year everyone has something he or she doesn't want for Christmas. For example, the one thing my wife doesn't want to find under our festive spruce is sexy lingerie.

Garter belts that light up and say, "Hello, sailor!", bras that were recently advertised in the back pages of a magazine titled *Saucy*, undies so miniscule the days of the week can only be embroidered on a corner in shorthand—well, Mrs. Lautens will have no part of them.

Unless they can come up with see-through flannelette, or a peekaboo bra that can fit over a cosy T-shirt, underwear manufacturers can forget it. The Resident Love Goddess passes.

As for me, the one thing I don't want this Christmas is anything that will make me smell nice, or provocative, he-man, macho, wealthy, secure in my masculinity, or like Joe Namath.

Don't get me wrong. I don't want to go around either giving off more fumes than the locker room at Maple Leaf Gardens. Armpit City is not where I want to reside.

What I want to smell like is nothing. Neutral. When I walk into a room I want nobody to notice. Does that explain it?

I want people to get right up beside me and still not have a nostril quiver, an eye blink or a libido perk up and paw the ground.

In short, I want to come through the holiday season without a scent to my name.

In recent years there has been a real push to get men to spray themselves with cologne, pre-shave, after-shave, skin bracers, bath splash and deodorant with more perfume than a parlour full of whoopee girls.

Unfortunately, the campaign to make males smell like an English saddle, a lavender bush in the French countryside, a spring day in Romania, a Roman orgy, or hay cut at dawn just east of Regina has been successful. In fact, it's so successful you can't take your nose anywhere any more without it keeling over in about four seconds flat.

Never in the history of the world have so many men given off so many fumes.

Now I'm not shy about my nose. To be frank, it's a real honker. Turn me upside down and I could pass for a Hoover. Okay, but the nose that has survived diapers, YMCA gymnasiums and winds blowing the wrong way off Hamilton Bay can't hack the aromas given off in a typically warm room these days.

At some of the parties I've been to lately you could cut the Scottish heather in the air with a knife.

Personally, I think it wrong, too, and mischievous when a person catches a tease of apple blossom only to find it wafting from a truck driver with a tattoo of Barrie on his arm. And there is always somebody named Harold who believes if a dab of bluebell is sexy, half a bottle will turn the evening into something even Hugh Hefner would envy.

But the main point is this: with the amount of talc, bath beads, perfumed soaps, etc. that will be left under Christmas trees this year for Hubby, Good Friend, Dad and so on, we could have the ultimate scent explosion.

By refusing such gift items myself, I hope to make the world a less smelly place in which to live.

No expiring nose will be able to look at me and with a last gasp mourn, "Et tu, Brut?"

Not Old Spice either.

December 21, 1981

107

Of mousse and men

The other evening we were watching "Moonlighting" on TV and I innocently mentioned to Mrs. Lautens that the best part of the series was when Cybill Shepherd ran in her slit skirt. At least once in every program, Cybill Shepherd runs in her slit skirt. In the best programs she falls down and shows even more of her legs.

"Don't men ever stop looking at women?" Mrs. Lautens asked. "Don't they get tired of looking at the same old thing?"

"No," I said.

Mrs. Lautens sighed in that little way she has that indicates disapproval. "Animals," she said.

"Thank you," I replied.

Well, why kid about it? Men are absolute saps when it comes to women. They will climb mountains for women, swim oceans for women, even vote for Brian Mulroney if it will please a member of the opposite sex.

Let me tell you how far a man will go for the love of a good woman. (Who said, "About half as far as he will go for the love of a bad one?")

A friend of mine's daughter spent the past year in France doing all the things kids tell their parents they are doing in France; i.e., studying culture, learning French, and definitely not partying it up every night.

Halfway through the year, my friend got a note from her daughter. It made two main points: (1) She needed a few things, including a favourite brand of mousse apparently unavailable in France; (2) If mother would buy said articles, the daughter's boyfriend would fly them to Paris where they were planning a wonderful reunion after months of being apart.

Mother (my friend) got the mousse, etc. and put them in a blue suitcase which was picked up by the boyfriend on the way to Pearson airport.

The boyfriend was a little put out by the size of the suitcase. After all, he had only a little back pack himself. It was also his first trip to Europe.

But with visions of the wonderful girlfriend waiting for him at the other end—Paris—he kept the grumbling to a minimum.

Let us quick-forward a few hours. The boyfriend has arrived in Paris and he is waiting for his luggage to come down the ramp.

He notices the baggage area filling with soldiers but, with all the international scares, he puts it down to regular security. After all, it is his first trip to Europe and he speaks no French.

Suddenly he sees the blue suitcase come down the ramp. Foam is coming out of it. The foam is blue.

As he reaches for the blue suitcase, a small platoon of soldiers surrounds him. Guns are trained on him. Orders are barked at him.

Ugly moments follow. He is scared. Finally, a fellow passenger explains (in English) what the authorities are saying. They think his suitcase might be a bomb.

The boyfriend explains the suitcase contains hair mousse for his girlfriend and opens it to prove he is only a person in love, not a terrorist.

The police are satisfied and finally leave. The young man is just about a nervous wreck after his ordeal.

Finally, a half-hour late, his girlfriend arrives. He tells her the story. She laughs her head off.

He does not strangle her. See what I mean about love?

September 15, 1986

Women get to me — for these reasons

Twenty-five things about women that bug men:

1. They won't order dessert no matter how much you encourage them, but when the waiter brings you your banana cream pie, carrot cake, etc., they always want "just a taste."

2. They always wait until you are just about asleep before they want to have a meaningful conversation about something bothering them.

3. They fall asleep immediately after meaningful conversations (see above) while you toss and turn.

4. They make you eat broccoli.

5. They think a swell way to spend a Saturday afternoon is to go downtown and look at furniture.

6. They want to turn off the office air-conditioner even if it's boiling out.

7. When you say, "What do you want to do tonight?", they say, "I don't know, what do you want to do?"

8. When you are driving the car and they have the instructions on how to get where you are going, they say, "Turn here," when you are even with the intersection and there is a lane of traffic between you and the turn.

9. When you are going out, they want to put bulky things (lipstick tubes, combs, tissue, etc.) in your pocket so they won't have to carry a purse.

10. They make you change your tie before you go out.

11. They leave hair in the bathroom sink.

12. They do not see the artistic merit and dramatic nuance in films featuring Sylvester Stallone, aliens from outer space bent on world destruction, or any movie in

which the featured players remove their clothes as an integral part of the plot (for example, *Swedish Co-Eds Go Berserk*).

13. They like Sissy Spacek movies.

14. They make you stand in the express checkout line at the supermarket even though you have 11 items.

15. They love to watch TV close-ups of actual heart operations and other icky surgical procedures, but they wince when you peel an orange with your teeth.

16. When you bring home a fish wrapped in newspaper given you by somebody at the office, they act as if you've handed them a bomb instead of tomorrow's dinner.

17. They expect you to keep track of all the cheques you write.

18. For some reason, they find Tom Selleck attractive.

19. Thanks to male stereotyping (I blame the media), they expect us to be able to explain what constitutes a balk, an automatic out under the infield fly rule, and where to find the spare tire in the new cars.

20. They practically have to be dragged home before the dancing starts at the annual company dinner-dance.

21. They can just look in your face and tell if you're up to something.

22. They do not throw a good spiral.

23. If you tell them more than 5,000 times that your mother was a saint, they get sore and tell you to knock it off.

24. They do not like you messing their hair if you get home late from a game the Blue Jays have won and are feeling good.

25. They always leave the car seat so you bump your knee the next time you get in.

Of course, none of the above applies to my Life Partner, who is perfect.

October 3, 1986

25 things about men that really bug women

Your agent is astonished. A couple of weeks ago I innocently listed 25 things about women that bug men. Now women are writing to say men aren't perfect either. Frankly, the thought never occurred to me.

Janice Sharwood Caldwell and Wendy Ashton Shimkofsky sent long letters about men. I've had telephone calls. Even my wife has chipped in with her two bits worth.

Here, apparently, are 25 things about men that bug women:

1. They want you to get all dolled up to go out and then get mad when other men look at you.

2. They leave the toilet seat up.

3. They think a chef's salad for dinner means you're mad at them.

4. They act as if the world is coming to an end if you get a new hairstyle.

5. They refuse to ask directions no matter how lost they are.

6. They think you still darn socks.

7. They get angry when you hammer nails into the wall even though you cover the split plaster with a picture.

8. They won't jog with you.

9. They never close closet doors.

10. They can sleep through a baby hollering its head off, but if you snore just the teeniest bit they grump and poke you in the ribs.

11. They are incapable of matching clothes even with the lights on.

12. They want you to go with them to the doctor's.

13. They expect you to go to their office party but com-

plain they don't know anyone if you ask them to yours.

14. They make snide remarks when you watch "Dynasty."

15. They buy you underwear that is totally uncomfortable and are hurt when you don't wear it.

16. They always get romantic about four minutes before the company is due to arrive.

17. They have at least one sweatshirt that should be taken out and shot, and buried 15 miles from the nearest community.

18. They think it's fun to rub their whiskers on your face before they shave.

19. They are always trying to toss things (apple cores, rolled-up tissues, etc.) into the kitchen garbage pail from about 10 feet away, and missing.

20. They are sure they're dying when they've got a simple cold.

21. They insist on keeping the temperature in the bedroom around freezing and then can't understand why you don't wear the sexy nightgown they got you last Christmas.

22. They refuse to take anything back to the store for a refund. They don't like paying for anything with coupons, either.

23. They actually like breakfast.

24. They handle every domestic crisis with the same three words, "Ask your mother."

25. They are absolutely certain every male friend you have is just waiting for a chance to throw you over his shoulder and carry you off to the Whoopee Motel (water beds a specialty).

26. . . .

Well, the list goes on, but the space here doesn't, thank heavens.

October 17, 1986

We scored a perfect 10 with this cuddle

Some men want to climb Everest, fly to the moon or get a $250-million contract from Ottawa.

I aim higher.

My goal in life has been to experience the perfect cuddle.

Last Wednesday morning at 7:12 a.m., all of my dreams came true.

I had the ultimate cuddle—a 10.

Every morning when the alarm goes off at 7, Mrs. Lautens and I have a cuddle before we plunge into the day. It has been our rule for 30 years.

In all that time, our cuddles have never fallen below a solid 8; most have been 9s.

But the miracle 10 has always eluded us—until last Wednesday.

The alarm went off, the 7 o'clock news came on, and we automatically began to snuggle.

At first I though it was going to be a 9, but then I realized it was better than that. A 9.5? Well, it seemed a record cuddle was within my grasp.

The room was just cool enough. The comforter was just cosy enough. I was at that perfect point midway between being awake and being asleep. The legs fit together just right.

That's when it began to dawn on me.

A 10 was definitely within reach.

For one thing, my arm didn't go to sleep as it sometimes does when a morning cuddle goes wrong. There were no sharp toenails to spoil the cuddle. My chin (which is pretty pointy) didn't dig into Jackie's shoulders nor did I have a morning sneeze without warning.

That was when the cuddle hit the miracle 10.

I said, "Mmmmm," and Jackie responded with "Hmm-mmm."

For at least 12 minutes we didn't move. All I could think was, "I don't want to ever get up. I'm going to stay like this forever."

Finally, just to make sure I wasn't imagining the perfection of the cuddle, I said to Jackie, "Is this the best cuddle the world has ever known, or what?"

Mrs. Lautens replied we were experiencing the cuddle to end all cuddles. It was the way man and woman must have felt when they saw their first sunset or touched their first flower.

"If there was a Nobel prize for cuddles, we would be the co-winners," I stated. "Edison when he discovered the electric bulb couldn't have felt this good."

Alas, like all perfect things, the perfect cuddle had to end.

There was breakfast to make, bath water to run, clothes to throw on, morning papers to read, major issues to worry about, money to be earned, garbage to take out, teeth to be brushed, appointments to be kept, telephone calls to be answered, elevator buttons to be pushed, traffic to be dodged, crowds to be shouldered, fast lunches to be bolted, notes to be written, people to be talked to, bills to be paid, cheques to be written, governments to be worried about, important news bulletins to be digested, supper to plan . . .

In short, there was life to go on.

Since that glorious morning, we have had our usual wonderful cuddles (a couple of 8.5s, the rest 9s) but we haven't attained perfection again. Perhaps we never will.

The perfect cuddle is so fragile. A seasonal cold, too much light, a cramp in your leg, a lump in the pillow that turns out to be the TV changer, a snore—they can spoil it in a split second.

If you ever do attain the perfect cuddle, though, remember this—you can only be second.

March 9, 1987

The women in my life don't take orders

Let me say right off the bat I am happy with the women in my life. Said women—namely one wife and the same number of female offspring—are tops in my book.

I cannot help but wonder, however, if I am missing out on something.

According to feminists, women have been dominated by men since that first fatal bite of Granny Smith in the Garden of Eden.

Not only have they been dominated, they've been manipulated, oppressed and generally ordered around by males.

My question is simple: Where are these women?

I have tried since old enough to bark out an order to dominate the women in my life. It has never worked.

My two grandmothers absolutely ran their homes and my grandfathers. They were tougher than Hulk Hogan. Even in their 70s, nobody would cross them.

My maternal grandmother (a Methodist) wouldn't allow any alcoholic beverage in her house and I have seen grown men sneak into her basement in order to grab a few clandestine drags on a cigarette behind the furnace.

My paternal grandmother weighed no more than 95 pounds and, pound for pound, was the most powerful person in the world. Even dust would fall upward in her home when Sophie gave it her stare.

If anyone ever manipulated them, it must have been while

I wasn't looking.

My own mother was just over 5 feet tall and she smiled all the time. But if she made up her mind about something, nobody on this earth could move her—except her own mother, of course. My mother made Churchill look like a guy who couldn't make up his mind.

And that brings me to the present women in the family—wife Jackie and daughter Jane.

Ho, ho, ho, don't let their bright smiles and winsome curls fool you. There are three men in the family (me, sons Stephen and Richard) but we would never be dumb enough to take on the women. They would wipe the floor with us, but not wax it, mind you, waxing being against their religion.

If I just once came in the house and said, "Woman, fetch my slippers!" the following would happen:

1. Nothing.

2. I would have the slippers stapled to my face.

3. My house key would be taken away and I'd be told to go to my room until I learned a few manners.

It wouldn't be pretty.

What I'm saying is, in my life I have only dealt with strong women, the kind with, ahem, firm chins, the kind that wouldn't put up with a temper tantrum or a snotty remark from the likes of me, the kind that can't be pushed, or pushed around.

In fairness, they don't go around giving you an Indian wrist burn or putting on a headlock when you aren't looking. They are easy to live with, sunny of disposition and can never get all the way through Bambi without tears. Jackie's strongest word is "darn."

But weak, bossed around, playthings of male masters?

Shere Hite obviously has never surveyed our home. If she did, the first thing she'd be told is to wipe her feet.

January 8, 1988

Damsels in distress! And here to save the day—our White Knight

Males have all kinds of fantasies—sexual, athletic, financial. But the most fundamental fantasy of all is the hero fantasy.

No matter our age, we dream of saving old ladies from burning buildings, of beating up gangs of toughs tormenting little pussycats, of rushing in with the mortgage money just as the bank is about to foreclose, of snatching beautiful maidens from fates too ugly even to discuss.

In short, in our hearts we see ourselves as heroes.

Unfortunately, because of the dragon shortage and whatnot, it is not always possible to fulfil a fantasy in today's society.

Still, there are moments when little triumphs are possible, when knighthood can at least bud if not flower.

For me, such a moment arrived Monday afternoon. And on Bloor Street of all places.

It was 4 o'clock. The weather was ideal for hero work—sunny, warm. The track was fast.

Even better. There were lots of witnesses.

Oh, that's very important in derring-do. You don't exactly want to blow your own trumpet, but it is nice to have a crowd on hand when you pull off some wonderful feat, some death-defying act, etc.

I was walking in front of the ManuLife Centre when I observed not one but two (2) members of the opposite sex in distress. Yes, a double-header of desperation.

There are two sets of double doors at the entrance of the building and a young mother was struggling valiantly to get into the building with a baby carriage while another young mother was trying to get out under the same circumstances (i.e., with a baby carriage).

It was the kind of situation a neo-Galahad dreams of, if you get my drift.

Both mothers and both carriages (containing lovely babies) were so wedged between the doors it looked as if they might be stuck there till spring—unless, ta-dah, someone oblivious to his own personal safety leaped to the rescue.

Enter your agent.

Out of the corner of my eye I saw life's drama unfolding. I saw the confusion as the mothers tried to figure out whether to pull, push or dismantle their carriages to get them past the doors.

Without a word I rushed to their aid.

Alas, a funny thing happened to me on my way to immortality.

I tripped over the step to the entranceway.

Mind you, I didn't exactly fall and sprawl all over the sidewalk or lunge headfirst into the distressed parcel of mothers.

But I stumbled in a performance that would rate a 5.8 for artistic interpretation even from the Russian judge.

By the time I regained my balance, the one mother had managed to pull her carriage into the ManuLife building and was staring at me with a look that said, "You're lucky you didn't kill yourself."

The mother coming out of the building took me by the arm and said, "Thank you for helping. Are you all right?" She was being sincere.

I mumbled something about being glad to be of help, and walked away.

I did not look back.

March 9, 1988

Fifty ways to (almost) please your lover

It started so simply.

I was talking to our youngest, Richard, about a birthday present for his mother.

"Your mother is turning 50," I said, "and I want to get her something special."

"Usually you give her lingerie," he pointed out. "It's sort of a tradition."

"I know but this is a special birthday. I can't believe it, but your mother is going to be 50. I need to get her something significant, something that reflects this particular birthday."

"You mean like 50 silver dollars or a 50-year-old book or something like that."

"Yes."

That's when the light went on between my ears.

"I know what I'm going to give your mother," I practically shouted. "I'm going to give her 50 pairs of panties."

Let the record show Richard said it was a great idea.

"Yes, 50 pairs of frilly, saucy panties," I repeated. "Each one different, each one representing a year of her life."

I couldn't believe I was so brilliant.

Without delay I went directly to Holt Renfrew on Bloor Street and practically galloped to the lingerie department.

"I want 50 pairs of panties," I told a clerk named Carol. "And I don't want any two pairs the same."

Carol burst out laughing.

"Nobody has ever asked for 50 pairs of panties before," she stated.

Of course, I was pleased to be the trailblazer.

"They're for my wife's 50th birthday," I said.

My wife, I informed Carol, was 124 pounds, 5 feet

7 inches. Then the fun began.

Panties began piling up on the counter. White ones, blue ones, pink ones, sophisticated black ones with loads of lace. A pair of red silk knickers in dance style was retrieved from an adults-only hanger. Ditto white knockouts that could have come from a Ruby Keeler movie.

You name it and it was in the collection—bikinis, innocent eyelet, Swedish imports, amusing patterns, one even with a little black bow at the back (presumably to be worn at black tie events).

I don't mind saying it was a collection of panties that could stack up against any in the world.

It wasn't until we were around the 40 mark in our panty fest that another thought entered my inspired mind.

What do 50 pairs of panties cost?

Sometimes I think that cement pole I ran into as a child caused more damage than the family thought. Anyway, belatedly I suspected I may have overlooked a flaw in my amazing idea.

After an hour of picking and choosing, Carol announced we had 50 pairs of panties and began cutting off all the little tags and totalling the bill.

According to the computer, we had exactly seven pages of panties.

Gulp!

Total cost was $780. Gulp! Gulp!

I hope the colour did not drain from my cheeks completely as I offered my credit card. I could hardly lose my enthusiasm, or change my mind, after what I had put everybody through.

The panties were gift-wrapped and duly presented to my wife at her birthday party.

Everyone seemed to enjoy my little joke, even Jackie's mother and father who have always figured I was a little nuts anyway.

Only one thing went wrong.

The panties are the wrong size.

May 23, 1988

If God were female, men's shirts would button at the back

There's been talk God is a woman.

What nonsense.

If God were a woman, the shopping carts at the supermarket wouldn't have wonky wheels, the shopping carts at the beer store would.

If God were a woman, the line-up would be in the men's washroom.

If God were a woman, men would have shirts that button at the back.

If God were a woman, every thermostat in the world would be fixed so they couldn't be set at less than 78 degrees Fahrenheit.

If God were a woman, the expectant father would throw up after breakfast.

If God were a woman, after every game the Toronto Maple Leafs would take a shower and get a leg-waxing, including bikini line.

If God were a woman, a person wouldn't have to take steroids to open a ketchup bottle.

If God were a woman, a man's haircut would cost $40.

If God were a woman, leaving the toilet seat up would be an automatic 60 days in the clink.

If God were a woman, it would be Wallabees that come with high heels.

122

If God were a woman, nuclear war, acid rain and sidewalk grates would be banned from the face of the earth.

If God were a woman, a female would be able to come home after a hard day at the office and shout, "What's for dinner?" as soon as she hit the front door.

If God were a woman, Rob Lowe would play Agent 007.

If God were a woman, there'd be a bill before Parliament right now providing free eye-liner to every female over 21 regardless of income.

If God were a woman, cellulite would never have been invented.

If God were a woman, there would be no birth control ban in the Roman Catholic church.

If God were a woman, men would be grumpy a few days every month—instead of all the time.

If God were a woman, Hamilton would come in another colour.

If God were a woman, men would have to walk in gift underwear that consists of a Band-Aid held together by two pieces of string.

If God were a woman, cottage cheese would taste like chocolate mocha layer cake.

If God were a woman, you could make a left turn from any part of the road, and no stick shifts.

If God were a woman, straight hair would never go out of style.

If God were a woman, every TV set in the world would self-destruct if tuned into a football game on a nice Sunday afternoon.

If God were a woman, shoe sizes would be standard throughout our solar system.

If God were a woman, PMS would stand for post-Mulroney syndrome.

If God were a woman, pitchers in the major leagues

would throw underhand.

If God were a woman, Harold Ballard's mother would have had a headache instead.

If God were a woman, there would be more men in the world bright enough to lift a chesterfield and chew gum at the same time.

If God were a woman, good girls would go to heaven, bad girls would get facial hair.

Finally, if God were a woman, there might be widespread conviction (to paraphrase Oscar Wilde) that in creating man, She overestimated Her ability.

November 21, 1988

Do we give kissing enough lip service?

I'm worried Canadians are forgetting how to kiss on the lips.

I don't mean social butterflies named Posey, Bimsey and Catherine who traditionally greet each other by putting their cheeks together and kissing into mid-air.

I don't mean showbiz types from Regina who, having seen too many old Paul Henreid films, like to plant suave smackeroos on the back of somebody's hand.

No, I'm talking about ordinary Canadians.

From mid-October to May, Canadians just don't go around kissing each other on the mouth. That's because it's the cold and flu season.

Unless you're absolutely dizzy in love, have lost your will to live or have a partner who moves just as you've lined up her forehead, no Canadian kisses on the mouth in January, or any month with an "r" in it.

First of all, you have a tickle in your own throat and want

to keep away from any loved one to spare yourself the guilt of possibly infecting them.

And if that's not the case, the loved one is sneezing loud enough to blow the doorknobs off the medicine cabinet and is in the untouchable category.

In my own personal case, for example, Mrs. Lautens and I have been alternating sinus infections, ache-all-over feelings and chest coughs since fall.

Whenever her nose is dry and germ-free, my honker is like the Gardiner Expressway in winter—wet, slippery and backed up to Oakville.

And when I'm okay, the Resident Love Goddess is throwing back vitamin C tablets in a last-ditch attempt to prevent a bug from Hong Kong or some other exotic point from setting up residence even in her hair roots.

I keep a diary and from my notes it appears the last time we kissed on the lips was on my birthday, November 3.

We were in London, England, on that day and got carried away with the occasion.

Of course, we were both sniffling within 48 hours.

What is a Canadian to do?

I go to the movies a lot and it is all right to watch Harrison Ford kiss Melanie Griffith on the lips, or to see William Hurt and Geena Davis pucker up for each other.

But it is not the same as kissing a person yourself.

Kissing is not at its best as a spectator sport. I don't care if the person you're kissing giggles, opens her eyes or even has a bit of toast on her lip, it is a lot of fun.

My own till-death-us-do-part has a little habit that can put a damper on a good kiss. When I go into the kitchen before supper and beg a kiss to tide me over, Jackie will set the timer on the microwave for five or ten seconds, depending on how busy she is, and give me the requested peck until the buzzer beeps.

I don't mind. A kiss with the right person is worth it.

But will Canadians forget the technique, the approach, where the noses go, in these non-osculation days of winter? Will kissing become a lost art, except among college students and teenagers who would risk kissing an alligator with measles on date night?

I hope not.

In the meantime, as they say in the suburbs, it's a long way between buss stops.

January 9, 1989

Thoughts linger of puppy love and youthful kisses

Forget the conflict and the anger. Lay aside news items of the awful things humans do to each other. Begone politicians and kings, generals and tycoons.

Join me in a toast.

Here's to long ago kisses and puppy love.

This morning I was talking to a friend at work. Happily married, father of two, nice guy.

I congratulated him on his birthday, which fell this weekend.

And I remarked how many people I know with birthdays at this time of year. I listed a few.

Without pause he said, "My old girlfriend's birthday was May 9." He then rattled off her telephone number, too—in Tokyo.

He was talking about a romance 25 years ago.

Men don't forget. They may forget their licence number, the name of the premier of Prince Edward Island, their shirt size or when they have tickets for *The Phantom of the Opera*.

They may even forget Dave Stieb's ERA.

But they don't forget old crushes.

Ask George Bush if you don't believe me. Mention it to Chairman Gorbachev the next time you see him on the street. Quiz any of the Reichmann brothers if you like.

We all remember.

I once took out a girl named Joan. "Our" song was "Don't Fence Me In" by Cole Porter. That was 45 years ago.

Do you want to know what Norma wore to class in Grade 12 when I thought she was the most wonderful creature in the world and almost had enough nerve to talk to her?

She wore one of those Jantzen sweaters (maroon) with animal figures. And a gray skirt, oiled moccasins, white bobby sox.

And she rode an old bicycle to school without a reflector on the fender.

I will provide her 1944 address on request.

At 16 I adored a girl whose birthday was September 19. Her middle name was Eunice. Not many people knew that. And one New Year's Eve we spent in a funeral home where she was babysitting.

See?

Men are sentimental about such things. I don't care if François Mitterrand is president of France. I bet he knows some foolish bit of trivia about a girl he worshipped in grade school. Maybe her dog's name. Or where he sent her letters in summer vacation.

Not even Finance Minister Michael Wilson is exempt. Tucked away among budget figures, flow charts and GST projects, I am sure he has a memory of an old flame from school days. Maybe just her bank account number or her mark in math class, but something.

Do women remember, too?

Does Elsie (whom I was dizzy for) recall how dapper I

looked in my orange cardigan with brushed wool inserts, my war surplus pants turned up at the cuffs, and my Dick Haymes loafers?

Does Barb go all atingle for a split second every November 3, recalling my birthday?

Frankly, I don't think so.

Women are more practical. They are too busy in the present to think about some goof who made moon eyes over them dozens of years ago.

Why, whenever I mention one of my wife's old boyfriends to her, she has trouble even calling up his name let alone other details.

A few weeks ago we were looking at one of Jackie's old high school yearbooks and came across a picture of someone who looked an awful lot like my wife kissing some boy at a school dance.

Not only did Jackie not remember the boy, she did not remember the incident.

I guess women have different memories.

Or are smart enough not to blab so much.

May 14, 1990

Let's put the lid on dangerous toilet-seat covers

You have never heard me criticize women.

I love women.

The way they look. The way they walk. The way they think. The way they laugh. The way they go to the doctor without a whimper. The way they have babies. The way they keep track of details. The way they feel when you hug them. The way they worry about you and make you eat vegetables.

I love women.

But they are not perfect.

I am not talking about how they want you to turn off the air conditioner even when it's 30 degrees Celsius outside. I am not talking about how they go all quiet when you (sensibly) want to drive non-stop for six hours to get to the cottage.

I am not even talking about how they want to answer a telephone just because it's ringing, even if "Murphy Brown" is on TV.

No.

I'm talking serious.

I'm talking toilet-seat covers.

Nothing on the face of the earth has cursed man more or forced him to assume more awkward positions than the toilet-seat cover.

Toilet-seat covers are useless. All they do is make it impossible for the toilet seat to stay in an upright position. If you do get it up, there is no guarantee it will stay that way.

I do not want to be more graphic, but keeping the toilet seat upright with one knee while you hop on one foot is not an easy task.

Back injuries among men would drop 75 percent if toilet-seat covers were banned. So would incidences of men pitching into walls headfirst and knocking themselves out.

It is obvious the toilet-seat cover was invented by a woman. No man would be suicidal enough to dream up something that would imperil his life and limb at such critical moments. Even the atomic bomb has an off-switch.

But women adore them.

Crocheted, padded, store-bought, pink and fuzzy, it doesn't matter. As long as they transform the toilet seat into a lethal weapon that will fall without warning, women buy them. They should walk a day in a man's moccasins, if you get my drift.

In my lifetime, I've had eight aunts. They all had toilet-seat covers on their bathroom fixtures. Aunt Nellie's always had more pile than the front room rug. You could hardly open the toilet let alone expect the lid to stay up.

My mother (who was a saint) had several toilet-seat covers, so even on washday, our toilet seat was never uncovered.

Any male who used our bathroom at 3 a.m. in the dark did so at his own risk. Management accepted no responsibility for personal accidents like dull thuds followed by profanity.

Of course, discretion is to be admired, but I have news for women.

You can cover a toilet seat with a toilet-seat cover featuring a flamingo or the Mona Lisa, but people will still guess what is underneath is a toilet. They will not think they are in Florida or visiting the Louvre.

So why not raise your right hand and repeat after me, "I will not put a toilet-seat cover on any toilet seat in the house, even when there's company coming, so help me American Standard."

Trust me. You'll get a standing ovation.

Do as I say and you'll be perfect.

June 6, 1990

If it hurts to be in love, you better dump the thug

According to a study reported in yesterday's paper, 25 to 35 percent of young women perceive violence as a sign of love.

Are they nuts?

Violence is not love. Any time, anywhere, any way.

130

Here are signs of love:

Likes lots of nice hugs and cuddles.

Scratches your back after a long day.

Wallpapers the living room on his day off.

Thinks it's great when plans for Saturday night fall through and he can spend the evening just with you.

Won't take you to scary movies because he knows you hate them.

Says you look great when you need a little lift.

Worries if you have a tough day at the office.

Takes your side. Always.

Loves to cosy up Sunday morning in bed with you and the weekend papers.

Knows all the lyrics to "your" song.

Holds the umbrella over you when it's raining even if it means he gets a little wet.

Puts up with this obsession you have to feed him broccoli.

Likes to pat you on the bum whenever he gets a chance.

Thinks you're really smart and can do everything from managing money to curing the rash on his arm.

Remembers your first date in detail, including how nervous he was to meet your parents.

Tries to make you laugh.

Pays for parking when you're wearing high heels so you won't have to walk so far.

Goes for hand-holding in a big way.

Doesn't pout when you say Tom Henke is your favourite Blue Jay even though he thinks Joe Carter's Number 1.

Likes you to help pick out his clothes.

Knows enough to keep quiet when you're feeling blue.

Lets you hold the TV changer now and then.

Stays cool when you shave your legs in the bathtub; doesn't make a scene over the residue fuzz.

Lets you have a bite of his dessert when you're on a diet

and don't order one yourself.

Buys you lingerie on any excuse.

Never leaves the toilet seat up.

Pretends not to notice if you get a pimple on your face.

Limits himself to one or two jokes a week about your father.

Gives you little winks from across the floor when you're separated at parties.

Wants the kids to have a lot of their mother in them when they grow up.

Makes a goofy face now and then to lighten the day.

Doesn't sneak up behind you and push you into the lake after you've complained it's too cold.

Can't understand what you see in him but is awfully glad you see something.

Never wears plaid pants.

Likes to end each day making spoons and saying, "Good night, sweetie."

Finally . . .

Wouldn't hurt you for the world.

That's a sign of love.

Where do people get screwy notions that hitting someone is love?

Weird.

August 23, 1991

Sizing up a woman may baffle mere male

I have been buying women's clothes for 40 years.

Stop tittering.

You know what I mean.

If you prefer, I have been buying clothes for womenfolk on their birthdays, at Christmas, for anniversaries.

And I still know absolutely nothing about the subject.

I know what I like. I know what looks good. I know what is in fashion.

I pay attention to such things.

But what I don't know, and never will, is women's sizes.

As far as I'm concerned, women's sizes are just as deep a mystery as nuclear fission, global warming and Ken Russell movies.

They beat me.

Here is an example.

My wife is about 5 feet, 7 inches tall. She weighs 124 pounds. As I've mentioned, she has not changed over the years.

Her going-away outfit (bought for our 1957 wedding) still fits perfectly.

In short, we are dealing with a pretty stable body, a body which after 35 years I should be able to buy for without scratching my head and saying, "Duh."

But it isn't that way.

This is what I mean.

The other day Jackie went shopping for a straight black skirt for work. No big deal.

She returned home with the skirt.

It was size 9-10.

So the Resident Love Goddess is a 9-10, right?

Wrong.

Jackie also saw a lovely green skirt she thought I should buy her for Christmas. The fact I wasn't there is incidental. Jackie didn't want me to miss a chance to get a start on my Christmas shopping just because I was home at the time. Besides, it was 30 percent off.

So what size was the green skirt?

It was a 6.

That's right. The black skirt was a 9-10, the green skirt a 6.

Same woman. Same body. But three sizes different.

Do only men think that's nuts? I wear a 42 jacket. It is always a 42 jacket. It isn't a 38 jacket, a 48 jacket. It is a 42 jacket.

You can buy me a jacket anywhere and it is always the same size. My pants don't change size. My shirts don't change size. My shoes don't change size.

Why can't women's sizes be the same?

How can we shop for them when sizes are all over the place?

And the green skirt, the size 6?

Jackie decided I was really into the Christmas spirit and bought the jacket that goes with it.

Was it at least a 6?

No, it was a 5-6.

Is this crazy, or what?

Men like to buy outfits for women but how can anyone figure out what size to look for?

I have returned so many items of women's wearing apparel because of a size problem, I now refuse to shop anywhere unless they give cash refunds.

And there are millions of men just like me.

Women have to get their act together.

Figure out this size thing.

I'm lucky my wife has been able to finish my Christmas shopping for her early this year.

At least I know everything fits.

So that's it. No more shopping.

Okay, maybe a teddy—but only if the sales clerk is built approximately like my wife.

December 9, 1991

5

What Is a Canadian?

Seasonal look at Canadian character

Out of respect for the season, herewith a list of Canadian definitions for January:

A Canadian motorist is someone who drives the first 25 blocks on any car trip trying to see through the one inch of clear windshield above the defroster vent.

A Canadian humanitarian is somebody who will expose his face long enough to tell you your nose has turned white.

A Canadian only puts his foot down to shake off the snow.

A Canadian feminist is somebody who will shoot pucks at a garage door with you.

A Canadian businessman is somebody who doesn't smile in public in case he gives the impression things are going okay.

A Canadian hockey coach is a person who can work "you know" into a sentence during an interview at least 27 times without taking a breath.

A Canadian Don Juan doesn't show the depth of his affection by sending flowers and candy—he makes the supreme sacrifice of getting into bed first to warm up the sheets. In Canada, this is called foreplay.

A Canadian fashion plate carries her shoes to smart parties in a Ziggy's bag, and rolls up her long johns so they don't show below her Mirror Room dress.

A Canadian watching a Hollywood version of winter at the movies always nudges his companion and points out it's fake because you can't see the actors' breath.

A considerate Canadian is someone who has a bench

in his front hall so you can sit down and take off your galoshes.

A Canadian is somebody who faces a big decision every time he goes to a place like Maple Leaf Gardens—whether to wear his coat or stuff it under his seat on the floor.

A Canadian parent is somebody who, no matter how much he practises, is always two seconds late in undoing his four-year-old's snowsuit.

A Canadian patron of the arts is somebody who waits for loud music or laughter in the theatre before coughing, sneezing or using nasal mist.

A Canadian immortal is somebody who has lived through three Winnipeg winters, preferably consecutively.

A Canadian husband, in a lasting marriage, is willing to be first downstairs in the morning to turn up the thermostat.

A Canadian would sooner be caught dead than without a paper hankie in his pocket.

A Canadian's age can be determined by counting the salt rings around his or her boots.

A Canadian philosopher ponders deep questions like, "Are there snow tires after death?", "Where does the sky go in winter?" and "How will people in Edmonton know when the next Ice Age arrives?"

A working Canadian actor is somebody who lives in Los Angeles.

A Canadian thinks a "slush fund" is a jar where you keep money for dry cleaning.

A Canadian embrace is when your goose down is pressed against her goose down, and your Chapstick brushes against her Lipsaver.

Finally, a Canadian is somebody with his shoulder to the wheel, also to the fender, the front grill, the bumper . . .

January 8, 1982

English, French can live together just fine, *merci*

I've done some dumb things in my life, but perhaps the dumbest is buying a cottage in Quebec.

The cottage is 600 kilometres from Toronto. It takes nearly six hours of hard driving to get here.

Because of the hard winters, the water pipes crack and split if we're not careful. Beaver chew our trees, our dock tilts at a crazy angle because of last year's ice, mountain storms often knock out the power.

So why not sell and move closer to T.O.?

Because I have this love affair with Quebec and the French.

I've always liked Quebec City and its elegant streets. I've liked the graceful way the Montreal Canadiens play hockey. I've liked French food, fashion and *joie de vivre*.

When I was a young sportswriter, the road trips I prized were the ones to Montreal.

And I like my French neighbours at the lake.

The other day I had to get a plumber to drain out the water system, not an easy task from 600 kilometres away. All I had to do was call my neighbour Pierre Langlois. He made the arrangements and made sure they were carried out.

When we move to the cottage (we put in about six weeks total over the average year), we get invitations from Julien and Rolande LaCroix for tea.

Gilles Racine and Hélène will paddle over or invite us for a gourmet dinner.

Robert and Marcelle Taché are quick to arrange some social evening at their home or some little restaurant they have discovered.

It is a very special part of our life.

They help us with our French and we help them with their English (although they are far better with English than we are with French). Conversation switches back and forth.

We talk about the lake, our kids, work, our concerns.

For the last couple of Bastille Days, we've arranged a party. This summer it was our turn to host and Jackie did a meal in the colours of the French tricolour—*bleu*, *blanc*, *rouge*. It was a great evening.

What I'm saying, I guess, is that we get along and like each other a lot.

That's why I get annoyed when the politicians barge in and start making speeches filled with threats, gloomy predictions and stern warnings.

They don't speak for me.

I get along fine with André Dagenais at the hardware store. The visit to Pagé for bread is always a joy. The man at the deli counter at Provigo has been giving me a friendly wave for at least 10 years.

And when I try to order lunch in French at Le Jardin, everyone laughs.

In short, I feel at home in Quebec. It is my real home for part of the year, and always in a corner of my heart.

It is no accident I have a series of four photographs on my office desk. They are views from the porch of our Quebec cottage.

I do not have pictures of Brian, Bourassa, Manning, Parizeau or any newspaper columnist, East or West.

I think Canadians could get along all right with each other if the politicians would just shut up for a year or so.

In the meantime, we'll still play "Ode to Joy" on the car tape deck when we near our Quebec cottage. It's a tradition with us.

November 6, 1989

Let's close the language gap — one word at a time

I know how to save Canada. I know how the French and the English can get along better and become friends.

It's easy.

We have to speak slower. We have to enunciate better. And we have to make sure we don't slur our words.

I'm not joking.

The reason Quebec and the rest of the country are always grumbling at each other is communication.

We don't understand what each other is saying.

The French think the English should learn their language. And the English think the French should speak theirs.

Okay.

But the fact is many Quebecers did take English at school, and vice versa.

Unfortunately, we speak our own languages so fast nobody can understand what we're saying.

I took seven years of French at school, yet I am left behind when Quebecers wind up and start talking. It's like trying to step into a car that's going by at 60 m.p.h.

If Quebecers would cut their word output by even 25 percent, I would catch their drift. So would most English-speaking Canadians who have gone through our school system.

The same is true for Quebecers when they hear us jabber away in our language. We talk a blue streak and they feel left out because they can only pick out an occasional word.

What we have to do is set up slow-speaking schools across the nation.

The schools would teach Ontarians, for example, to avoid sentences like, "CanyoubelievethatMulroneyguythewayheslapsontaxesandwhataboutthoseLeafs, eh?"

That is fine, if you were brought up in T.O. We follow perfectly. But a visitor from Montreal's east end would be baffled and feel like a stranger from another planet. No wonder he wants to set up another country.

A slow-speaking school would fix that. It would make us put in pauses, say complete words and order us to stay after four if we run paragraphs into a verbal blur. It would turn out students who speak English a Quebecer could understand.

Obviously, Quebec should do the same. There could even be scholarships for the slowest-speaking students in each province.

Of course, there would be crackdowns on slang, buzzwords and sports announcers who do play-by-play of an entire period in hockey without taking a breath.

Personally, I like the way foreigners talk English and French. They are easier to understand because they go slow and follow the textbook.

It's a great joy when you can understand a foreign language. If we all speak slower, soon Quebecers will flock to the Soo, and Thunder Bay residents will be booking trips to Quebec City—both feeling completely at home.

As starters, politicians should set an example. No long words in their speeches. No attempt to cram an extra verb or two into the 30-second TV clip. And present tense if possible.

We will be embracing in 10 years.

I promise.

February 7, 1990

Bring your dreams to Canada, but not old feuds

Advice to immigrants:

Bring with you your skills, energy, hard work and brains.

Bring your dreams.

But leave behind old feuds and scars.

Canada is not a battleground for your past. It is the hope for your future.

We are all newcomers here.

Never forget why you came to Canada. For a better life.

Never forget why you left your old land. Because it didn't hold the promise you sought for you and your family.

Love your old country.

But love Canada more.

It is all right to be nostalgic about old customs and old ways of doing things.

But you cannot expect to make a new life and have new friends if you do not change. You have to accommodate.

Learn the language. Learn the ways. Appreciate the wonderful gift that is Canada. Do not treat Canada like a mere cash register. Do not expect love if you give none.

Demand clean air from Canada, and safe streets. Demand good schools. Demand equal opportunity. Demand respect. Demand decency.

Do not demand a free ride or special treatment or instant success. It takes time.

Travel.

See the mountains, the rivers, the plains.

Visit the cities, the farmlands, the small towns.

Feel the country.

When you know Canada, you'll realize it is even more wonderful than you thought from the brochures.

We are blessed. Share the joy. Share the good fortune. Watch the news at night and read the newspaper—then say a prayer of thanksgiving.

Get involved. Do not retreat into some ethnic island away from the mainstream of Canadian life.

We are a little bit English, French, Hungarian, German, American, Chinese, Greek, Italian, Portuguese, Japanese, Caribbean, Indian, Vietnamese, Australian, Ukrainian, Dutch, Scottish—and dozens and dozens more.

Aren't we lucky?

We can enjoy it all without leaving home.

Bring the best from your homeland but leave behind what didn't work. We need no passion for lost causes and futile grudges.

Read history. Understand why Canadians like the United States but do not want to be part of it. Understand why French-speaking Canadians have been in this land 400 years and feel threatened. Understand what the English have contributed to our way of life.

Understand why cold winters and drought, depression and hard times, have made the West suspicious of bankers, Bay Street and fast-talking feds.

Understand the sadness of the native people. Understand the struggle of the Atlantic provinces to survive.

They are good people. They have their reasons. Do not judge them too harshly or too quickly. They may be right. Their fear of change can be understood. Some change may be wrong.

Finally, laugh.

This country sometimes gets too serious. We worry a lot.

So bring us your gifts of enterprise and intellect, your kids and your courage.

But bring us your laughter, too.

We need that.

One final note: My grandfather, Franz Lautenschlager, came to this country nearly 100 years ago.

I think it was the smartest thing he ever did. So did he.

April 4, 1990

Considerate, orderly and discreet—so Canadian

Sometimes I see something and say to myself, "Boy, that's so Canadian."

Three examples:

Example One: The other day I was walking through the lobby of the ManuLife Centre on Bloor Street.

In the lobby there are several bank machines.

There was a line-up for the machines.

The line-up was long. It was straight. It was orderly.

But this is the part I liked:

The line-up was a discreet 10 feet from the people using the machines.

It was so Canadian.

Canadians don't want to look over your shoulder when you are transacting business even with a machine.

Nor do they want their shoulder looked over.

So they keep a polite distance.

Whether you're depositing or withdrawing, whether it's $10 or $1,000, whether you're paying a bill or transferring from chequing to savings, Canadians do not want to get too close.

Money is personal.

Money is private.

Money is nobody's business but your own.

So Canadians stay well back—even on a Friday afternoon when they are in a hurry.

I like that about us.

Example Two: I was at the last Blue Jays home game and it hit me—I have never seen a single person break the no-smoking rule at the SkyDome.

Not a single puff.

Here we have almost 50,000 people in a stadium and they all follow the rules.

It's so Canadian.

Sure, they smoke where they're allowed—away from the seating area.

But not in the seats.

Can you imagine that happening in New York City? Can you imagine 50,000 Frenchmen not lighting up? Or Brits? Or Italians? Or anything?

Of course, the rule makes sense.

Smoking in a domed stadium would stink up the place in no time and turn everyone brown.

But the point is, you can go to SkyDome and see 50,000 Canadians with their butts on seats, not hanging from their lips.

It is unique.

I am not sure it could be duplicated anywhere else in the world.

Example Three: I was walking down Yonge Street with my daughter when a young girl came out of a pizza store.

She began munching pizza.

And then she dropped the cardboard pizza plate to the sidewalk.

Plop. Just like that.

What did I feel the urge to do?

Of course, you know.

Tap the girl on the shoulder and tell her (sweetly), "Pardon, you dropped this cardboard pizza plate."

And then hand it back to her in all innocence as if doing her a big favour.

It's so Canadian.

Alas, I didn't do what I wanted to do. I didn't give her a lesson on the spot about littering and keeping the environment clean.

That's also so Canadian.

Aren't we funny?

I'd say more, but that would be bragging. We don't like bragging. In fact, if I've said anything to offend litterers, smokers, users of bank machines, bank machines, minority groups, our good friends in other lands, equal rights activists, I apologize. Sorry. I take it all back. . . . It's so Canadian.

October 22, 1990

Where will Quebec get the money for its destiny?

Forget the bold speeches. Forget the macho stances. Forget the strutting and posturing.

Let's get down to cruel facts. Quebec says it is now free to assume its own destiny.

Fine.

Who's going to pay for it?

I ask not in a mean way, not in a nasty way.

I just ask.

According to a University of Calgary study by economists Robert L. Mansell and Ronald C. Schlenker, Quebec has been running at a loss for 20 years.

From 1961 to 1988, Quebec got $136.4 billion more from Canada than it put in.

From 1980 to 1988, Quebec's gain was $95 billion—$1,600 profit per Quebecer per year.

That's from equalization payments, subsidies from Have to Have Not provinces.

That's from the federalism Quebec politicians and media are so quick to criticize.

Not bad.

Please don't think Quebecers are the only beneficiaries. Residents of Prince Edward Island got nearly $5,000 per person in the same time.

The difference is, P.E.I. is not talking about independence.

So we go back to the point.

How will Quebec make up this shortfall in cash?

What happens when Quebec doesn't enjoy the profit of Alberta oil, Ontario manufacturing, British Columbia timber?

What secret piggybank will Bourassa rattle?

Will he cut social benefits subsidized between 1961 and 1988 with $136.4 billion of other people's money? Old age pensions? Baby bonuses?

Where will he get the huge grants that brought helicopter, automobile and other industries to *la belle province*?

I have no clue and Bourassa offers no help.

Apparently he wants to share some things with Canada —banking, currency, the army.

He also wants to continue sending MPs to Parliament. Lucien Bouchard and other political pals will not join any unemployment line.

But are Albertans prepared to pick up some of Quebec's tab as they have for 20 years?

While Quebecers were getting back $1,600 more than they were paying each year, Albertans were sending $4,200 more to Ottawa than they were getting back. This is a hard world.

What's in it for Ontario if Quebec wants to go its own way? For B.C.?

Does Bourassa realistically expect Canada to contribute still to an independent Quebec's unemployment fund?

Dreams are expensive.

But nobody in Quebec ever talks about cost. Come to think of it, nobody in Ottawa talks about cost, either.

Let's put numbers on the table.

The last time there was a separatist wave in Quebec, thousands of people moved out, businesses left, property values went down.

The same feeling is there today.

A neighbour of mine moved out of Quebec in the last spree—and took his factory and 140 jobs with him.

So cut out the flag-waving, the breast-beating.

Where is Quebec going to get the cash to run its own show?

I ask without malice.

Quebec has been running in the red for 20 years.

You can't pay bills with another rally or even a press release.

September 7, 1990

Storm a sure cure for what ails Winter Weenieland

At last. Real Canadian winter.

No more of that wimpy stuff.

You know—temperatures above freezing, ducks bobbing on OPEN water, not even slush in the streets, let alone good "packers."

It's awful.

We're Canadians. Our breath is supposed to come out in white puffs. Our feet are meant to be cold and wet. Our noses are designed to go numb.

It's guaranteed in the Charter of Rights.

Toronto has looked like a big sissy resort town so far this winter. Okay, a few days when you might want to wear a scarf.

But how many igloos have you seen on front lawns? How many mitts have been piled on your hot air register? How many times have you almost broken your neck on the front steps?

Right—practically none.

We're getting soft.

I haven't pushed the car a single time this winter and my fleece boots in the basement might just as well be a centre-piece for the dining room table for all the use they've been.

This winter storm came just in time.

Gasping for breath over a snow shovel, getting the kids bundled in snowsuits so they can make angels in the play-ground, discussing whether this is the winter to resume skating.

You forget how to do those things if you don't keep in practice.

Besides, we need blizzards, cold spells, traffic-stopping snowstorms and Arctic fronts that chill to the bone.

We need them for our mental health.

In a typical Canadian winter, we spend hours talking about the weather.

How long it took to get home. How much the heating bill costs. How thick the ice was on the windshield.

It fills the winter months for Canadians.

But without sub-zero temperatures and snowdrifts, we look around for other things to grouse about.

We grumble instead about the government, the economy,

the situation in some country we never heard of before.

Before you know it, we start feeling sorry for ourselves. We go around saying, "Poor us," and, "Aren't things just awful?"

We just have too much time on our hands, time that in a normal winter could be used building an ice rink in the backyard, shivering in front of a fire after street hockey, or looking for a toe rubber in the Canadian tundra.

Instead of winter pursuits, we listen to politicians and watch CBC documentaries about how we're all doomed.

I think that is what has happened to us this winter.

We've spent too much time wringing our hands instead of our socks.

A good winter scares off the faint of heart. It gives us a chance to understand Mother Nature and appreciate our gifts. It provides an excuse to look at strangers and bond with them by saying, "Cold enough for you?"

This is what we are—northern people.

This isn't a country for weenies.

Snow and blow. That's our role. That's our game.

Believe me, the storm came just in time. Our brains were beginning to melt and our hearts turn to mush.

January 15, 1992

Let's think of our duties

Every day we read about people demanding their rights.

Their rights to housing, medical care, a bigger piece of the Canadian dream, day care, pets in apartments, self-government, better public transit, hot lunches at school, etc.

That's fine.

We all say, "Hurrah!"

But nobody ever talks about responsibilities.

We have a Charter of Rights.

Why not a Charter of Responsibilities?

This is a rough outline.

It is the responsibility of every Canadian to work, to pay his way, to contribute to society. Life is not a free ride nor should it be. There are no passes.

It is the responsibility of every Canadian to treat others with decency and respect.

It is the responsibility of Canadians to act as if their mother were watching.

It is the responsibility of every Canadian to keep his temper, watch his language and make sure he isn't a nuisance.

It is the responsibility of Canadians to keep their drinking under control. That goes for other habits that affect all of society, too.

It is the responsibility of every Canadian to pay attention to his health. If you mess up your life, everyone pays because you can't function properly.

It is your responsibility to get education, training, a trade — something to make you useful.

It is your responsibility to create, protect and cherish beauty in the world.

It is your responsibility to do the best job you can raising the kids. The world does not need youngsters with no values who consider the world an enemy and life a loveless place to raise only hell.

It is your responsibility to help others to the best of your ability.

It is your responsibility to respect what past generations have left us, and make sure future generations have reason to thank us.

It is your responsibility to set a good example. More people are watching than you imagine.

It is your responsibility to try to stop smoking one more

time. It ruins your lungs and puts a definite damper on your kissing appeal.

It is your responsibility to have some enthusiasm for life. Don't go around like a sourpuss always looking for something to frown about.

It is your responsibility to fight war, disease, hunger, illiteracy. It is your responsibility to make this a kinder world than you found it.

It is your responsibility not to get too big for your britches. If you don't realize how little you know, you aren't very smart.

It is your responsibility to be a good friend to nature and the world we are privileged to inhabit. Look at the stars at night and feel the magic.

It is your responsibility to solve as many of your problems yourself without automatically turning to the government.

It is your responsibility to use your head for more than a place to put a hat.

It is your responsibility to watch government spending as if it were your own—which it is.

It is your responsibility to be a sucker now and then. Better to be taken advantage of because you have too much heart than to take advantage of someone else because you have too little.

It is your responsibility to be fair.

It is your responsibility sometimes to say things to people they don't want to hear. Be gentle when you do.

It is your responsibility to look for the right way, not the easy way.

Finally, it is your responsibility to give a little more than you get. Or at least try.

January 7, 1991

Unity row seems trivial when a friend is in danger

I got a letter this week from a good friend of mine in Quebec.

Bad news.

His wife has breast cancer and is recovering from surgery, chemo and the rest.

Of course, it hit his family like a ton of bricks. They're very close, the kind of family that has dinner together, attends church together, plays together. Very traditional.

My friend's wife is a knockout. Bright, funny, a gourmet cook, no airs, exquisite taste, a good mother, a devoted partner.

Best of all, they are truly in love.

And now this.

My friend says they are going about life as normally as possible, hopeful of a happy ending.

Then he added in his note:

"Something like this makes you realize what is important in life."

I've thought a lot about that line.

My friend is French, his family has been in Canada for generations, and he (like all of us) has been caught up in Meech Lake, separatism vs federalism, Spicer, Allaire and all the other commissions.

Often when we are together in the summer, we talk about such things. We exchange points of view. We sometimes disagree.

But something like this—cancer—puts life into perspective. It sets our priorities right.

When the life of a loved one is on the line, does it really matter very much what some bank president says about economic viability? Do you hang on statements from the lips of some politician in Ottawa, or Quebec City?

Does it matter if the latest polls are up or down, if anthems or flags are jeered or cheered?

Not very much.

It doesn't matter what language you speak.

When sorrow comes, we all cry the same way. We all lay awake with open eyes wondering what's hit us.

There is no culture gap in cancer. There is no difference in the test tube. We are all mortal.

We all waste time worrying about unimportant things. We talk about differences that appear when you simply cross a line on a map.

It's as if we come from different planets and have hearts with different beats.

That's how it seems when you read the paper, watch TV or listen to speeches.

Parizeau makes jokes about Anglos having no emotions. Anglos fire back French has no business on corn flakes boxes.

We argue over words. We argue over fine print.

What a waste of time. What nonsense.

Ask my friend whose wife has cancer.

In a few weeks we will be back at the Laurentian lake where we have cottages. We will talk about politics. We will talk about leadership. We will talk about separatism and federalism.

But we will also talk about important things.

We will talk about our families. We will talk about being afraid of his wife's cancer. We will talk about the sweetness of life.

And when we talk, being French or being English won't seem very important at all.

May 3, 1991

Let's start a country—and we could call it Canada

I have an idea.

Let's start a country.

This country would have bright leaders in politics, labour, business, education and other fields.

They wouldn't squabble. They wouldn't call each other names.

They would try to get along.

In this country people would work hard—and they would be allowed to keep a lot of their money.

Oh, they'd help out the handicapped, the old, the sick, those who have been thrown out of work for no fault of their own.

But no freeloading.

You couldn't sit around twiddling your thumbs, abusing your body, making trouble or just being a nuisance.

You would have to carry your share of the burden and not expect somebody else to always look after you.

You'd be responsible for your life—and no running away.

You'd have to be useful.

In this country you'd respect other people and they'd be expected to respect you. You could not sit around griping all the time or making a lot of demands.

If you made a mess of things, you'd be told to look for the culprit first in a mirror before you started pointing a finger.

You'd have to follow some rules because this country would work best that way.

For example, you'd have to keep your mitts off other people, unless in affection. No abusing animals either, or property, or people's dreams.

You'd be asked to understand things like feelings and hopes.

Kids?

In this country kids would be special and need a lot of love and peanut butter sandwiches and talks. In return, they'd be expected to go to school, learn something useful and not be smart alecks.

They could keep pets provided they looked after them.

You'd be expected to cherish this country and treat it kindly. You'd be expected to understand its riches—and make sure something was left for the next generation.

And no putting it in second place to another country.

You can get sentimental about some holiday place, or a country in your past, or something you saw in *National Geographic*.

Of course, it's permissible to get dreamy about Paris, too. Everyone does.

But this country would be top priority, Number 1, your very own place, home.

You'd feel good about other people from your own country, even if they were a little different. You wouldn't act like a goof and insult them or treat them in a way you wouldn't want to be treated.

This country would have a nice touch of pride—but pride in important things like integrity, intelligence, cleanliness, decency and being fair. It wouldn't get a big head about things that are just luck.

What else?

I think I've left out fun.

This country should have lots of fun because life isn't much without it. You wouldn't want a country where everyone has a long face and snaps about the littlest thing.

You'd want to hear laughter. It's about as important as sunshine.

No idlers. No bullies. No grouches. No ingrates. No

shouters. No sourpusses. No crybabies. No parasites. No hotheads.

Yes, let's start a country.

We could call it Canada.

September 11, 1991

Who needs the Senate? Politicians — that's who

This is a really dull column.

It's about the Senate.

Personally, I'm skipping right to the sports page, but if you want to plow on, that's your business.

Brian, Joe and the gang want to "reform" Canada's upper house to make it "elected," "effective" and sort of equal.

Forget it.

Why don't they just cancel the whole thing.

The Senate, I mean.

Who needs it?

Politicians, that's who. Only politicians.

They like it because it provides work for their profession. Maybe "work" is the wrong word. It provides pay and perks.

And at taxpayers' expense.

Beauty.

You notice, over 10 percent of Canadians are out of work.

But politicians never have layoffs.

Theirs is the only profession in the land that hasn't experienced a single layoff, even one firing. If there is a mandatory early retirement plan in politics, I haven't heard of it.

Politicians enjoy a full 100 percent employment rate even in the kind of recession we're experiencing.

But back to the Senate.

Prime ministers like a Senate so they can reward their friends — and their friends like it as a nice retirement plan.

I say nuts.

The Senate should be abolished and the money used for the living and useful.

If politicians get tears in their eyes when contemplating a Senateless world, here are three alternatives.

1. Hand out Senate appointments — but make sure they don't come with a pay cheque, an office, a secretary and an airline pass. That way "distinguished" Canadians can still be singled out and called senator, but it won't cost taxpayers a dime.

There is no flaw in proposal Number 1, but if that's not good enough . . .

2. Let's hold a Senate lottery. Every Canadian over the age of 16 would be eligible for a two-year term as a senator.

Names would be pulled out of a hat to select members of the Senate. In their term of office, winners would get present Senate benefits — subsidized meals, cheap haircuts, chance to meet the Queen. Even dinners with Conrad Black.

It seems to me Canadians would become pro-Senate if they thought they had a chance personally to benefit from their own tax dollars.

If that isn't acceptable, I proceed now to . . .

3. Leave the old system in place — but with this one change.

The Prime Minister and his inner circle could still appoint senators, but the candidates could *not* be old politicians, academics, backroom plotters, pollsters, newspaper people, relatives, defeated candidates, etc.

In short, politicians would have to appoint senators from real people — farmers, factory workers, computer programmers, mothers who work, mothers who stay home, students, guys who fix your car at the muffler shop, real estate agents, ex-athletes . . .

Well, you know — civilians.

It seems to me if politicians really believe in a Senate, they would go with one of my three plans.

If they stick with their present thinking, it seems to me all they're doing is making sure no politician in this country goes without a job — and a photo opportunity.

And handing us poor saps, the taxpayers, the bill.

October 2, 1991

Please tell me what native people mean by self-rule

I'd like the newspaper to do me a favour.

Explain Indian demands for "self-rule."

We carry stories all the time about the Assembly of First Nations asking for "native self-government" or "aboriginal self-rule."

And it's fashionable to nod and agree.

But I honestly don't know what it means.

Do Indians want their own country?

Do they want territory with their own capital city, parliament, senate, civil service?

Would it have customs, post office system, diplomatic corps?

Would there be an army, navy and air force?

And the big question.

Would Indian self-rule mean native people would collect their own taxes and pay their own way?

In other words, would they be on their own and never ask Ottawa for another dime?

That, to me, is what self-rule means.

You can't have a truly independent nation if you're on somebody else's payroll.

I don't ask in any smart aleck way.

I just don't know.

I read about native self-rule, I listen to it discussed on TV programs, I watch Indian leaders make speeches about it.

But I don't know the nuts and bolts of what they're demanding.

Should I be politically correct and say it's wonderful, has a lovely ring to it, makes a lot of sense?

Or should I say forget it?

I don't know.

That's why I'd like this newspaper to do a story. A simple story, one with no fuzzy phrases, one that gets down to the meat and potatoes.

What is native self-rule?

Is it dual citizenship? Is it going to require passports? Will an Indian nation have its own bank and currency? What will it cost us—or save us? Have native people voted for it?

What land are we talking about? Show me a map.

Are native leaders talking about a form of apartheid, a society of their own cut off from Canada? Or a society within a society?

Well, there are a hundred questions in my mind.

Native self-rule? It goes on and on. Never concluded. Never resolved. Always adjourned to another day.

What am I missing?

Are all these conventions just an excuse for photo opportunities? Who pays for these meetings? Is it just a lot of hot air?

Or are we talking about another Quebec?

I'd love to see a balance sheet on Indian self-rule. What are the costs? What are the implications to the native living on a reserve up north, or the one who has made a career in the city?

Please, no lawyer talk. No novel-length summation by a bureaucrat. No harangue by an activist with an axe to grind.

Just facts.

About 800 words.

Pros and cons.

No punches pulled.

I hate to break the news to Joe Clark and Ovide Mercredi, but Canadians are tired of trying to figure out exactly what they're talking about.

December 6, 1991

No political sex scandals, please — we're Canadian

Twenty-five reasons U.S. politicians have more sex scandals than Canadian politicians:

1. Teddy Kennedy is on their team.

2. Too darn cold in Canada to take off your clothes.

3. Canadian reporters aren't nearly as good as American counterparts at digging up the juicy stuff.

4. Tories would rather make money.

5. NDP would rather spend money.

6. Liberals would rather call another conference to talk about money.

7. Because of GST, PST and other taxes, cost of an affair in Canada is out of reach for the average politician.

8. Canadians now do cross-border hugging and kissing in cities like Buffalo where sex is cheaper even with the duty.

9. Canadian politicians spend too much time attending

national unity conferences to have spare evenings for the opposite sex.

10. The U.S. got all rights to seduction in the free trade agreement by clouding our negotiators' minds with strong drink.

11. With the Leafs only 11 points out of a playoff position, who has time to think about sex?

12. Bob Rae says we can't afford it.

13. Canadian politicians are occupied arguing about how much sex Quebec should get if they separate.

14. The best offer any supermarket magazine has made to a Canadian woman for revealing her affairs with one of our politicians is $12.

15. No training film available at present.

16. Canadian politicians are too busy taking holidays in Florida to spend time searching the streets of Moose Jaw for companionship.

17. Canadian women just laugh when our senators ask them to play strip checkers.

18. Our public leaders don't want to waste their puckers on shady females when they can kiss up to Brian.

19. We've spent all our money wining and dining Jack Morris and other Blue Jays.

20. Sex is part of the American tradition in public life. Our leaders talk to dead dogs.

21. Many Canadian politicians have strong religious convictions and are afraid sex could lead to dancing.

22. Sex isn't on the Constitution agenda.

23. The Tories aren't dumb—they know only 12 percent of Canadians will go to bed with them.

24. Sex in the U.S. gets a spot on "60 Minutes." Sex in Canada would mean a 12-part series on CBC titled "Sex in Ottawa—What Does It Mean to Native Land Claims, Pay Equity and Our Relations with the Third World?"

25. U.S. politicians don't have the excitement of Joe Clark speeches to distract them.

January 29, 1992

O, Canada! We have lots to appreciate

Time out.

For the next three minutes forget the complaints, the faults, the problems.

No sad songs today.

Let us count our blessings as Canadians.

We've got a vast land filled with natural resources, bustling cities, gorgeous mountains, prairies with sweet earth as far as you can see. We've got oceans to fish and more than our share of blue sky.

We have Nature as our friend.

We have the benefit of many cultures—especially the British tradition of law and order, the French *joie de vivre*, the American go-get-'em enterprise.

Nice combination.

No secret police knock on our doors in the middle of the night. No mobs roam the streets. Our courts are not run by colonels in backrooms.

We are outraged by injustice. It is not a luxury all people enjoy.

We have social programs. No one starves to death on our streets. We have health programs. The system cares.

Our schools have books and trained teachers. Kids can dream big in Canada.

No government censor decides what goes in our newspapers. There are no secret jails awaiting commentators who say too much.

Politicians squabble in debate. Disagreement is a right, not a privilege.

You can go to any church you want. Or no church at all. You can do just about anything you want—provided you don't hurt others.

Children aren't sent into the mines, grown-ups aren't herded into factories like animals. We have rules.

Of course, there are bumps, examples of meanness.

But there are battalions of men and women ready to ferret them out and expose them. Canadians prize fairness and decency. They do not take lightly the exploiters.

We have interesting weather. No one-season year for us. We have cold and warm sunshine and long nights, soft summer days and winter winds that can cut through board. It is never dull, never predictable.

We also have interesting people: Oscar Peterson, Karen Kain, Norrie Frye, June Callwood, John Polyani, Gretzky, Pierre Trudeau, Donald Sutherland, Lynn Johnston, Lincoln Alexander, Milt Dunnell.

And many, many more. All special. All us.

We have lots of ordinary folks, too. Hard workers. Raising families. Paying their way. Saying "eh?" at the end of their sentences.

Good solid people who mind their business.

Canadians.

We have food on supermarket shelves. Telephones that work. Shots for polio, flu and dozens of other things. We have big cities like T.O., Montreal, Vancouver. But we have St. Mary's, Ontario, too, and Morden, Manitoba.

Nice.

I have Hamilton, and the walk along the mountain brow, and a restaurant named the Troc I've been going to for 40 years, and a hospital where my three kids (and wife) were all born.

You have your hometown, too. A special place. A safe place. A place where memories live.

All good.

Pollsters say Canadians are depressed right now. They say we're discouraged.

Don't be. Think of all the good things we have. Think of how lucky we are.

To be Canadian.

November 4, 1990

I Just Want to be Perfect

To be perfectly frank, I just want to be perfect!

I'm tired of being human.

I'm tired of being flawed, of being dumb, of having a pimple break out on my face on the day of the party.

I want to be perfect.

I want to have all the right answers, I want to do all the right things, I want to think all the right thoughts.

I want to know how to solve terrorism, to come up with a plan to provide everyone with a job, to produce housing young people can afford. I want to know how to speak 38 languages, and play the piano, and talk brilliantly about Freud and Beethoven and Dwight Gooden.

I want to know how to fix a kitchen tap, canoe through rapids, dispose of nuclear waste, eliminate acid rain, fix a 10-speed bike when the chain comes off, take a picture that doesn't chop off the heads of half the people.

I want to know what to wear with a checked jacket. I want to understand computers. I want to be able to flip menacing bullies with my little finger. I want to get along with foreign countries and solve differences over lunch. I want to rattle off all Ira Gershwin's lyrics by heart. I want terrific posture.

I want to be a knockout parent. I want to be wise when my kids come to me with their problems. I want to be soothing when I should be soothing, firm when I should be firm, and to know the difference.

I want to have perfect breath and a body that everyone says looks as if it were carved from marble. I want to dance like a dream, tell funny jokes and be a fantastic lover.

I want to have the knack of thinking of something clever to say at the right moment, not two days later. I want to be on everybody's A list.

I want to eat ribs without getting grease up to my shoulders. I want to write marvellous paragraphs that people remember and quote. I want to be fun at picnics, school reunions and office parties where the bosses couldn't help but remember my name. I want to be an ideal friend.

I don't want to screw up, to stumble and trip my way through life. I don't want to buy high and sell low. I don't want to forget the punchline halfway through the joke.

I don't want to snore, lose my hair, catch colds, forget to signal my turn or laugh in the wrong place in a movie. I don't want to step on anybody's toe, burn hamburgs on the barbecue, scrape the side of the car, or have to wear eyeglasses.

I don't want to get the wrong answer, forget a name, arrive late, walk around with my fly unzipped, lose my temper, or speak sharply to somebody because my mind is somewhere else.

I don't want to hang pictures crooked in the front room, drop in on somebody when they're eating, get the new baby's sex wrong, make the wrong turn on the highway, or get liver spots on my hands.

I just want to be brilliant. I just want to go through life without a false step. I want to be able to recommend quaint little restaurants in Paris, to knock off a painting when I have an afternoon free, to jog 10 or 12 miles before dinner to sharpen the appetite, to take Ann Landers' call when she has a personal problem.

Alas, it isn't to be.

What I retain from my classroom days at university you could put in a thimble. I get weary by 11. My knee clicks. My hair is thin. My disposition is often the pits. I forget to return calls. There are a thousand things I wish I had said to people when there was time, and a thousand kisses I should have given them. My brain is too often out to lunch. I can't hit the curveball.

I'd really like to be perfect.

May 12, 1986

Airport security leaves no brim unturned

I have gone through many security checks at the airport. My pockets have been emptied, my luggage X-rayed, my armpits prodded, my in-seam scrutinized, my hotel towels sniffed by Dobermans.

Nothing about me, I assumed, had escaped the sharp eye of the men and women who stand guard at the nation's air terminals asking for your boarding pass.

I was wrong.

A couple of weeks ago at Terminal 2, Lester B. Pearson International, while preparing to go bye-bye to Winnipeg on a Pacific Western supper flight, I was asked to remove something I've never been asked to remove before by an airport security person.

The guard (female) asked me to remove my hat.

She wanted to see what I had underneath.

As long-time readers of this column know, there is nothing under my hat. Never has been. But the guard wanted to see for herself.

After the inspection, I began to think about the little episode. Was I asked to remove my hat—a fur job I've owned 12 years—purely on the grounds it is of Russian manufacture and was purchased by your correspondent in Leningrad?

Have the Mounties issued a bulletin to airport guards asking them to be on the lookout for subversive hats, left-leaning fedoras, Marxist peak caps, etc.?

Is some terrorist group now making bombs size 7¼, with ear flaps?

Or do airport security people automatically assume that anyone wanting to fly to Winnipeg in the winter must be (a) nuts, (b) a terrorist, (c) at the Winnipeg gate when he's really looking for the plane to Nassau?

Here are 10 other reasons why the security guard may have asked to look under my hat:

1. The RCMP has added a dandruff section to its national security force.

2. One of the security guards bet co-workers $1 she could get the next passenger to take off his hat and look like an idiot.

3. The guard wanted to make sure the fur hat was dead and not the family pet being smuggled on board the plane without a ticket.

4. She wondered if the Davy Crockett craze was back and was checking to see if the hat had a tail.

5. She was looking for fleas.

6. An all-points bulletin has been issued for a member of a Satanic cult who had escaped prison, and she wanted to check the top of my head for an obscene tattoo.

7. The guard felt I looked awfully warm under the fur hat and was only asking me to take off the handsome bit of haberdashery so I'd be more comfortable.

8. She heard Harold Ballard was in the terminal on his way to a Leaf road game and wanted to make sure he didn't slip through her station incognito without signing an autograph.

9. The guard gets turned on when men take off their hats and was looking for a cheap thrill.

10. She didn't want me to frighten any of the children in the airport.

Happily, my hat got full security clearance and made the rest of the journey to Winnipeg without incident. Me, too.

December 1, 1986

Lautens' family seat exposed to the world

I was raised in a family that believed a man should keep his pants on in mixed company.

My mother (a Methodist) was quite strict about that. And my father, though in the newspaper business and a Scorpio, was just as fussy.

A well brought-up male person does not show his bum when there are ladies present.

It was an iron-clad rule in our home.

I wouldn't reveal these intimate details except they may help if you choose to continue with this story.

For some time I have been bothered with a rash that comes and goes. The rash is on my left buttock.

A few days ago I decided to do something about it.

I decided to see a doctor.

Now, for years I've had a succession of doctors who shared one common characteristic. They have all been male.

Of course this will cause a yelp, but I am more relaxed around doctors of my same sexual persuasion. By that I mean a male doctor at least has a 50–50 chance of dragging me into his office while I clutch desperately to his door jamb, shouting the pain has gone away.

In any case, I made my way to the family practice where we take our maladies.

I was just starting to explain my problem to a tall male doctor when a young woman walked into the consulting room.

The tall, etc. doctor explained the young woman was an intern, and would I mind if she sat in on our consultation.

Of course you are ahead of me.

At first I wanted to change ailments in mid-course, to say I was there for a sore throat, or perhaps a dinky knee— something I could share without getting all dry in the throat, and blushing.

But I couldn't think fast enough.

I had to admit I was there because of the rash on my posterior.

"Pull down your pants and show me," the doctor advised.

"Couldn't I just describe it?" I said.

The doctor said it would help a great deal if he could actually look at the rash.

Well, there didn't seem any way out so I undid my belt, figuring with my kind of luck, I couldn't realistically hope for an earthquake to strike at that minute and level the entire building.

The doctor wasn't satisfied. He wanted me to slip down my underwear, too, thus exposing the Lautens' family seat that had never before betrayed a mother's trust.

The doctor looked at my posterior. The young female intern looked at my posterior. They talked about it quite seriously, and I'll be forever grateful the young woman didn't giggle once.

When I commented it was a new experience for me, to her credit, the intern coolly said, "I'm a doctor."

If she is being marked on attitude, I hope she gets an A.

In a few minutes the examination was over and I was told I could pull up my pants, which I did with as much sophistication as I could muster at that point.

I have some ointment that I am to apply sparingly once a day and I am to report back to the doctor in a month.

In the meantime, that's one more Lautens' tradition down the drain.

May 5, 1989

I'm up to my ears in old Wallabees

Approximately 20 years ago, my feet discovered Wallabees. It was a case of love at first fit.

I loved the crepe sole, the soft leather uppers, the no-nonsense arch support. Even the infamous Lautens' baby toe (that curls under) was totally happy in the new housing.

Since then my basic transportation has been the Wallabee —black, moccasin style, medium width, size 12, made in Ireland, now $110 a pair.

I have worn them in all kinds of weather, to faraway places, on hikes, at the office.

As my wife will attest, I have also worn them to posh dances where, thanks to the rubber soles, I have had a perfect excuse not to dance.

What matter I look like a sociology professor at York, or a person who might be delivering advertising flyers door-to-door.

My Wallabees have never been far from the family piggies.

But now I have a problem.

I am drowning in Wallabees. I have Wallabees coming out my ears. I am being Wallabeed to death.

You see, Wallabees don't wear out.

They wear down, they curl, they get thin in the middle,

they turn white from the winter salt.

But they never really wear out.

They are the closest thing to indestructible the human mind has ever devised.

So when they get a few thousand miles on them and need to be replaced, a Wallabee owner doesn't know what to do with his old ones.

They are still too good to toss out, but they are not good enough to wear in the company of people who eat with a knife and fork.

As a result, a person like me winds up with a lot of used Wallabees.

At first, the challenge was easy. I merely put the original old Wallabees at the back of my closet for rainy days.

When I progressed to my third pair of Wallabees, I put the second pair of old Wallabees in the basement in case I needed shoes in a hurry to take out the garbage or clean the furnace filter.

When I hit pair Number 4, I left them at the cottage so I wouldn't have to carry shoes back and forth from home.

Pair Number 5 landed at the office, where I keep them in case I get wet feet walking to work in the rain.

Just the other day I bought a new pair of Wallabees and I am beginning to panic.

I now have yet another pair of slightly curled, down-at-the-heel, old Wallabees that turn white when they get wet — but still have some wear left in them.

I have run out of places to hide them.

Do I make a nuclear fallout shelter out of old Wallabees? They would withstand all but a direct hit, I'm sure. Or should I make them into a sculpture and sell it as a piece of art to the city, guaranteeing it will not only look as good as a lot of what passes for art these days but will last at least 1,000 years. I know not.

It's kind of spooky walking around in shoes you know will be around long after you're gone.

October 9, 1989

New glove preserves a family rite of fatherhood

It's now official. I think you can safely say I've entered my second childhood. My skin will probably break out next week.

There is no other explanation for what I did a few days ago.

I bought myself a baseball glove.

Is that nuts, or what?

Look, I am 61 years of age. At 61 you buy cardigan sweaters, chocolates with soft centres, prune juice in the Big Boss container, pin-up pictures of Muskoka sunsets, and fat dogs that waddle.

You do not buy baseball gloves.

At 61, even the Atlanta Braves won't look at you. The arm is gone. If you bend over for a grounder, bets are made whether you'll straighten up again. As for breaking up double plays with a good slide, forget it.

But I couldn't help myself.

I saw this sale of baseball gloves at Collegiate Sports and couldn't resist the urge to have one more ball glove in my lifetime.

My son Richard and I have been playing catch lately with borrowed gloves. Unfortunately, he had to give the gloves back to his friend Clegg.

So there we were — gloveless. And my curve just rounding into what now passes for shape.

Anyway, I got two of them. They're Cooper gloves, soft-tanned steerhide, Easy Flex Pocket, rawhide laced, Comfort Palm Pad. Cost: $59.99 each.

I've already put my initials on the back of my glove so it won't get mixed up with Richard's. Next we'll have to get some Neatsfoot Oil and work in a pocket.

It's the best glove I've ever owned. I've only had two.

When I was 12 I got my first newspaper job as an after-four office boy at the *Hamilton Spectator* in charge of baseball scores. The pay was $3 a week.

That was in 1941.

With that kind of money burning a hole in my pocket, I went to Longfield's Bicycle and Sport Shop on King Street where they had a baseball glove in the showcase.

The glove was gorgeous. A fielder's mitt with a little leather lace forming the pocket.

After some haggling, Mr. Longfield agreed to let me have the glove for $2.10, the exact amount I had in my pocket by coincidence.

Of course, Corky Rodwell, Bob Stimson and the other kids were impressed. You didn't see (new) $2.10 gloves every day at the playground.

I had the glove for years. Many summer nights my father and I would play catch in our side drive. He always wore a white shirt and necktie, dark dress trousers, slippers. He tucked his tie inside his shirt as his one concession to informality. And often he had a cigar in his mouth.

Then we'd throw the ball back and forth for a half-hour. Sometimes we didn't say a word.

He was a skinny guy, but he could whip the ball and never muss a hair on his head. My dad wasn't a person you could get close to (my mother claimed it was because he was a double Scorpio) but he loved baseball. He'd wind up and deliver just as if he were back in Elmwood in Winnipeg. Not many people ever saw that side of him.

Anyway, I have a new glove and it should last me till the ninth inning.

If you phone, let it ring a few times. I'm probably just out in the back lane showing off my submarine pitch.

May 4, 1990

It's better to give—unless you have to return it

There was a crisis in my life this week.

I had to return something to a store.

I hate that.

I'd rather have a cat with liver breath lick my face. I'd rather ride the Yonge Street bus after midnight. I'd rather listen to one of those weenie Ottawa commercials telling me how the GST is going to make my life better.

Perhaps I go too far. Especially on that last item.

But I do hate taking things back. Even with cause.

For my wife's birthday, good friends gave her a book— *Monet's Table*. It's a wonderful book. Has photos of artist Claude Monet's home at Giverny, recipes, menus at his daughter's wedding. Lots of stuff.

And, as readers who pay attention remember, my wife thinks Monet is the finest painter who ever lived.

The book, incidentally, is $39.95.

Now for the problem.

I got Jackie the same book.

And she opened their book first.

That, plus the fact I had the receipt, meant mine had to go back.

I don't know why, but any transaction where I'm getting a

refund makes me uncomfortable. A clerk just has to look at me and I'm sure she thinks I have used the product and brought it back. Or that I'm some kind of mindless cheapskate.

I can't haggle. It's embarrassing. I'm so bad with money, I should be an economist, or governor of the Bank of Canada. Does that say it all?

Exchanges are okay, provided they cost me more money.

In other words, if I give the clerk a bigger sale than the original one, I don't flinch. I can take a $40 item back, add $40 to it, and come out with an $80 article any time.

But take cash back?

It's beyond my ability to handle.

Of course, I've found a way around it.

I ask my wife to take back things I've bought but discover are duplicates, the wrong size, absolutely useless, etc.

But can you ask a wife to take back her own birthday present? Can you say to her, "Here's a book I bought but, since you've already got one, take it back and buy something else for yourself."

Even I don't have that kind of gall. Besides, the Resident Love Goddess might give me a Hamilton Beach kiss on the ear, and leave me deaf for a week.

For a few days I stalled. I told myself what with the Baltic states problem, Senate reform talk and Cineplex's disappointing first-quarter report, I just didn't have time to go to the store and, gulp, ask for my money back.

We also got a new issue of *National Geographic* featuring Austin, Texas, a city we all know too darn little about.

After about a week of lame excuses, I admitted it was time to screw up my courage and take the book back, even though I didn't know if the store had a refund policy. For all I knew, there might be a trap door in the floor at the cash counter where people who ask for refunds plummet into the mouth of a waiting crocodile.

Wait! There is a happy ending.

Just as life was at its darkest (I had the book as far as the dining room table), daughter Jane rode to the rescue.

She is visiting a relative and said the book would make a nice hostess gift.

Joy!

So the book is gone and I don't have to go through the agony of asking for a refund.

Jane paid cash, too. No credit slip.

May 21, 1990

What ever happened to the good old dog days?

It's a good thing Sarah the Semi Wonder Dog passed away a few years ago.

If she were alive today, she'd bite my ankle.

Couldn't blame her.

The reason is simple.

During her 14 years of life, Sarah could go anywhere she wanted in our house—except the living room. That was *verboten*. Off limits. *Interdit*.

Sarah knew better than to even look at the furniture let alone put a foot on the carpet. The line was drawn.

Okay.

So she hung around the kitchen, slept on the mat by the front door, occasionally climbed to the family room on the third floor. Mostly she stretched out on the front porch looking at people.

She was smart. She knew we wanted one room (out of eight) without any dog hair, a place where company could sit in dog-free comfort.

Now along comes Tigmund von Lautens.

Tigmund (also known as Tiggie) is a Bichon Frise pup, a gift daughter Jane received at Christmas.

He is about three months old, white and weighs 9 pounds.

He is my grand-dog.

And when he comes to visit (every Sunday) he is everywhere in our house.

Including the front room.

He plays with his toys on our front room rug. He tries to sniff candies on the coffee table. He even jumps up on my green chesterfield.

And no one says a thing to him.

Sarah in her entire life never jumped on the green chesterfield. All you had to say was, "Sar-ah!" and she would put down her ears and walk away.

Not Tigmund.

He struts around like a real somebody. He dashes down the hardwood and slides into the furniture when he fails to make a turn.

He has even been FED in the front room (by my daughter, not me) and told he's a good boy when he sits up for a bit of puppy chow.

What has happened to us?

Is this how people act when they become grandparents? Do all the old rules go out the window? Does your brain turn to mush?

Before Sarah, we had Geordie, a 200-pound St. Bernard. In 10 years he never treated our living room as if it were his own.

So that's a total of 24 years of dog ownership — and our pets were always perfectly behaved.

Along comes this pipsqueak and I'm afraid to sit down because he may be there first. It's nuts.

And bite?

Tigmund has teeth sharper than the instruments they used to take out my appendix. And he never stops using them.

What I'm saying is Tigmund gets away with murder.

When my wife calls Jane on the phone, invariably she's asked to speak to her grand-dog. "Tiggie, it's grandma," Jane says, holding the pup up to the receiver.

What's worse, my wife actually talks. "Hello, Tig," she says. Is that sickening, or what?

Poor Sarah never was put on the phone to anyone. As far as I know, she never received anything more than an occasional greeting card at Christmas or on her birthday.

Tigmund even gets praise when he goes to the bathroom INSIDE the house on newspapers.

I know I'm going to hear an eerie howl downstairs some moonless night.

It will be Sarah back to haunt us.

February 11, 1991

Great expectations are met at my first baby shower

Over the years I've been to political rallies, the World Series, stars' dressing rooms, Hollywood sets, Grey Cup finals, title fights, the Berlin Wall, the Olympic Games, Hamilton stags, castles on the Rhine, Viennese operettas, the Kremlin, and the Beatles' hotel room. I have even been to 24 Sussex Drive.

Brag, brag.

But one thing I've never experienced—a baby shower.

It never entered my mind that I was eligible for baby showers. Men of my generation just never were invited.

But a new age is here (I attribute it to the NDP government of Bob Rae) and a few days ago I attended my first-ever baby shower with other '90s kind of guys. Yes, a couples baby shower.

It's a good thing I haven't been attending baby showers over the past decades. If I had, I'd now weigh 600 pounds. That's because of the food.

Apparently, the big thing at baby showers (besides the expectant mother, of course) is the dessert table.

When men have a party, dessert isn't a big item. The only reason there's cake is to see who pops out of it and if she had a ride home, the animals.

But baby showers put a lot of emphasis on dessert. At this one, given by son Stephen and his wife, Rhea, for their friends Bill and Lona, there was:

Wine cake, coffee cake, brownies, gooey squares, fresh fruit, oatmeal cookies, icing with stuff underneath.

At a rough estimate, I'd say there were approximately 37,000 calories per guest.

I also found out there is a lot of audience participation at a baby shower. After every gift is opened, everyone in the room is expected to say, "Ahhhh!"

It doesn't matter if it's a cuddly bear or a diaper bag with leakproof pouch, you're supposed to say, "Ahhhh!"

I'm not sure but I think I ahhhhed at least 20 times; not bad, considering it was my first baby shower.

Then there's the conversation.

Okay, on this one I was a semi-washout.

Women have a language all their own when they get to affairs like this.

I didn't mind too much when they went into detail about false labour the mother-to-be went through a week ago. I could even fake interest about the hormonal mood swings that seemed to be a favourite topic of conversation.

But I did get a little woozy when they discussed in intimate detail the various parts of a woman's body involved in the birth thing.

You just have to say "uterus" and I'm out of there.

That, and a discussion about whether father-to-be Bill should actually cut the umbilical cord himself in the delivery room, caused me to remember something I had forgotten in the kitchen, where I stayed until a change of subject.

Forgive me. I don't want to know about some things in life.

The baby shower did end on a light note, however.

Apparently, it is a tradition at baby showers that the person whose gift is opened seventh will be the next one in the room to have a baby.

Guess whose present was opened seventh.

Yes, Mrs. Lautens'.

Everyone in the room got a laugh out of that. Well, just about everyone.

April 22, 1991

Mom worked 47 years before she got a pay cheque

I thought about my mother yesterday. It was Mother's Day, of course, but it was also my mother's birthday.

She would have been 83.

I can't believe it—83.

Bertha was always young to me. Well, she was only 20 when she had me. We were pals. Went to movies, ball games, hockey matches. I once took her to the Brant Inn when she won a date with Andy Williams.

She was quite a babe.

For no special reason yesterday, I thought about one of the high points in her life—getting her first old age pension cheque.

It was a special day.

To understand its significance, I have to go back a few years. My mother was from Morden, Manitoba, where her father did some farming without managing to accumulate the burden of wealth. In short, he had no dough.

When the family moved to Winnipeg, my mother was 16 and her school days were over.

She went to work for the *Winnipeg Free Press* and for two years knew the joy of a weekly pay cheque. My mother loved a bit of money. Every pay day she splurged on some treat for her family—candy, ice cream.

At 18, my mother married my father, who was being transferred to Fort William by his company, The Canadian Press.

Off they went into the horizon, bride and groom, to a city where they knew no one.

My mother never "worked" another day in her life. Oh, she cooked, cleaned, ironed, tended stubborn coal furnaces, shopped, did house repairs, cut the lawns, handled family bills, washed, waxed floors, etc.

But she never "worked."

Women of her generation didn't. They stayed home. They raised families. And they didn't get pay cheques.

My father was not a stingy man. He worked six-day weeks for his company for 50 years. In that time, he did not buy any yachts the family was aware of, nor did he ever smoke better than a 10-cent cigar.

We took in boarders for a few years, and my father also tried to make a killing as real estate mogul by selling a succession of family homes. Alas, he didn't make a wounding, let alone a killing.

But the point is, my mother depended on him for any money she got. He doled it out as an allowance. And while she said little, my mother didn't like being so dependent. That's the way the social system worked, though, and that's the way it stayed through depression years, World War II and on.

Let me mention there was a little extra in her pocket once I got work, but it was still a handout in her eyes.

Bertha only had her "housekeeping."

As she neared 65, my mother had two dreams: 1) to get a driver's licence; 2) to get the old age pension cheque—her own money.

We never knew but Bertha took driving lessons secretly and showed up on our doorstep one day with her licence.

It was one of her proudest moments.

Unfortunately, life doesn't always work as we plan.

Before she could take a car out on her own, spread her wings, so to speak, she got sick. She never did make it solo behind the driver's wheel.

The pension?

She did manage to get one cheque from the government and cash it. Her first very own money since she was 18 back in Winnipeg.

But that was all.

She never cashed the second.

That was in 1973.

I haven't forgotten.

May 13, 1991

J.L. was one strong-willed, uncompromising father

My brother has lived in Vancouver 28 years so we don't see much of each other but we do talk occasionally on the phone.

And talk, and talk.

186

The last time he called we talked one hour and 40 minutes.

Mostly we talked about our father—"Pop" to him, "J.L." to me.

Interesting man.

When he died in 1984, my (our) father was 78. Still tough. Still strong-willed. Still uncompromising.

J.L. left school at 15, but Trevor (my brother) and I have the same memory of his mind. Neither one of us ever heard him make the slightest slip in grammar. And if there was ever a dispute about spelling, J.L. was the final word.

He was meticulous about the language and, in spite of our high falutin' educations, we bowed to him. He was the champ.

He was also direct. He never wasted a word. He always went to the heart of the problem, discussion or whatever.

You always knew exactly what our father thought. He did not pull punches.

He didn't complain about work. He went to his job with Canadian Press in 1920 and stayed with the news agency until 1970—50 years. He worked six days a week, never made much money, but never griped either.

Trevor says he never heard our father whine or even discuss money. Me neither. All I know is J.L. figured being cheap was a capital offence.

Anyone who didn't pay his way was a "four-flusher." End of discussion.

Speaking of money, brother Trevor and I share another truth about our father: neither of us ever met anyone with so much integrity, if integrity has degrees.

As Trevor puts it, "Pop could walk through a room filled with gold coins and you'd know when he came out the other end, not a single coin would be missing."

The coins weren't his. End of discussion.

The man was untemptable. He would jump through no man's hoop. He didn't want a bigger home. He lusted after no promotions. He liked his own car (usually a second-hand Olds 88). He couldn't be reached by stroking his ego. Fancy suits, exclusive restaurants and the like sang no siren song in his ear.

And he spotted my mother when she was a kid of 16 and never looked at another woman until she died at 65.

He was just satisfied. Content.

He was a perfectionist in his work — technical stuff. He could throw a world-class tantrum or mood. And he was too strong for his own good. He was a black and white thinker.

After my mother died and he was alone, my father never quite adjusted. His world was never again the place it was. He had 10 hard years.

But he still maintained his spotless appearance. He kept his apartment immaculate. And you could still shave with his mind.

It was just different without "Bert," my mother, to provide the sunshine.

In the weeks before he died, he refused to go to hospital. He wanted to die in his own bedroom, surrounded by his things, and a family tree of photos. Of course, that's exactly what he did. J.L. always did it his way. No compromise.

He still managed to make it to the front room when we visited. And he insisted on putting on a shirt and tie to greet us, although he did wear his pyjama bottoms as a slight nod to his final illness.

The last time he saw my kids he shuffled to his bedroom and back, and slipped a $20 bill into each of their hands.

No four-flusher he.

Funny how long it takes to really know your parents and understand them. Trevor and I are still on that voyage and I'm 63 and he's 57.

Chicago banishes thoughts of work

If there's one thing I can't stand it's a good time. I can handle bad weather, political crisis, John Olerud's batting average and even the emptiness of knowing Brian is out of the country.

But good times exhaust me. Tire me out. Leave me brain dead.

At this moment you could shoot a cannon between my ears and not do any damage.

Blame it on my cousins in Chicago.

For three days we've been visiting them and for three days we've been doing nothing but have a good time.

We saw the wonderful impressionist art at the Chicago Art Institute. We went to the new Steppenwolf theatre to see an Albert Finney play. We drove by Mr. T's home. We ate ice cream in the middle of the afternoon.

Mrs. Lautens went to Saks and tried on goofy hats. We bought a cheap disposable camera at Wahlgreens. We leaned against the Wrigley building.

We went past Rock Hudson and Ann-Margret's old high school. We had dinner at Carlucci's. We browsed at Bloomingdales. We saw hours of family wedding videos.

We ate too much. We stayed up too late. We talked too long.

In short, we had a ball.

Cousin Diana even made us a fresh strawberry pie (with whipped cream) and Cousin Morley drove us around in his Mercedes.

Oh, how I love successful relatives.

But that is the up side.

The down side is I haven't a single clue at this moment on how to save the world, keep the nation together, salvage the Maple Leafs, balance the budget, put the Soo back on its feet, or improve our educational system.

In short, dear reader, you are not getting your money's worth today. You are paying the price for my little weekend.

Sorry.

The last time I was in Chicago was 28 years ago. At that time I gave you your money's worth. I sat in Al Capone's bathtub in the old Lexington hotel and scribbled about the experience. I interviewed Ann Landers and came up with a pithy 600 words.

I even bluffed my way into the site of the infamous St. Valentine's Day massacre and kept you on the edge of your seat with graphic details.

Not this visit.

I didn't go near a single public figure. As close as I got to a newspaper was walking past the *Chicago Tribune* building on my way to have a very nice lunch at a place called The Escargot.

Yes, I looked into the controversial Illinois state building —the one that's all glass and can't be heated or cooled—but I didn't make any notes.

Okay, here's the most damning confession of all.

The beloved Blue Jays were in Chicago for three games and I didn't go within three miles of the ball park.

Sorry I can't think of anything to depress you today or make you even mildly steamed.

My brain is out to lunch.

The only thing on my mind is my wife's raincoat. She forgot it in Chicago at the cousins'.

If we go back to retrieve it, my career will definitely be over. One good time a year is about all it can take.

May 22, 1991

The Boys of Summer fated to be boys all their lives

Here's a tip for women.

If they want to understand men, remember one thing: they never grow up totally.

They are always boys.

Maybe they have more expensive toys. Maybe they no longer put the knee out of their pants. Maybe they even learn not to use their sleeve for a hankie.

But inside they are still kids.

I thought about it this morning walking to work as I passed a school playground.

There, all by himself in a corner of the Church Street School playground, was a little fellow.

Maybe 5 or 6.

He was as intense as Bush at a White House cabinet meeting, as serious as the Pope delivering a speech from St. Peter's balcony, as dedicated as Conrad Black counting his money.

What was the lad doing?

He was trying to hit a ball.

Bat on his shoulder, he tossed the ball into the air with his hand.

Swing!

He missed by a foot.

He tried again.

Swing!

Another whiff.

I watched him try to hit that elusive ball three times. And three times there was no contact. Not even a little squib.

I don't know if the little boy will grow up to be a bus driver, a captain of industry, the Blue Jays' left fielder, an accountant or the discoverer of a cure for cancer.

He may also, dark thought, wind up as foolish as the two young men I saw the other day shooting dope into their arms at the park at our corner.

But he will never forget (once he learns) the joy of hitting a ball.

It is something the male of the species always remembers.

For some mysterious reason, hitting a ball is important to us.

I still remember 50 years back when we played ball in what was then the sports field of Hamilton's Cathedral High School.

Over the years I've had some high moments, but I'm not sure any accomplishment compares with the thrill of poling the ball over the left field fence on to Emerald Street and into the front yard of startled residents.

Man, did it feel good. You could tell up your arms when you got hold of one. You could hear the sweet sound on the bat. You could watch the ball sail into the air.

Wow!

Neighbours complained, of course, and often called the police when the ball bounced off their verandas.

But it was worth it.

Bob Stimson hit longer balls — but that left field fence for a few brief summers was mine.

What joy.

How lucky Joe Carter and Mookie Wilson and the others are to do it for a living. To have the talent to stay official boys just a little bit longer. To make jokes, sit in the sunshine, spit through their teeth—and hit a ball as hard as they can.

That's living.

I still dream sometimes about the thrill of hitting a ball right on the fat part of the bat and pulling it over some left field wall in my private never-never land.

Of course, I can't.

But, like that little kid in the schoolyard, I think about it —and wish about it.

Really dumb, eh?

Well, like I say, somewhere inside, a man never really grows up.

We just change our socks more often.

May 24, 1991

When I couldn't go to school, it drove me up a pole

Kids will hate this column. They'll hate me.

But I cannot tell a lie.

I liked school.

I liked my teachers.

Okay, my Latin teacher, Pop Devitt, could scare me with a look. And I had a French teacher, Muriel Paul, with a great arm who was clocked at 92 m.p.h. with a piece of chalk. She had great location, too, as Jerry Howarth would say.

But mostly, school was fun and I grew sad in June.

June meant I had to find a summer job.

In all those summers I never found a summer job I liked as much as school.

I worked in a factory—the National Steel Car—on shifts. I worked sorting T4 slips for the income tax people. I dug ditches.

None of it was a load of laughs.

The best summer job I had was working for the Hamilton Hydro and a man named George Oldham.

It was the summer of 1949, but I remember our crew — Ed Overholt, Pat Ryan, Paul Darouzet, Fergie Ferguson.

We put up transformers on hydro poles, replaced hydro lines and all that stuff.

The reason I semi-liked the job was because George Oldham took one look at me and realized instantly I was useless.

He was a kind man with a daughter who went to my old high school.

So he never asked me to do anything except load and unload the truck, fetch things for the crew up the pole and do minor jobs (on the ground) where I couldn't get into trouble like blowing myself up.

He also put me in charge of paperwork for the crew.

I made out time sheets, helped with requisitions for supplies and generally kept track of the office work.

As a result, I went back to university with all my body bits in one piece — plus enough money to pay my tuition.

Yea, George Oldham!

Blessed are those who are gentle with students not smart enough to come in out of the rain or work with anything hot.

By the time September rolled around each year, I couldn't wait to get back to school — to see old friends, to listen to Chester New lecture about the Great Reform Bill of 1832, to hang around the gym.

At school I could write a column for the campus newspaper, travel to out-of-town football games in a snappy Model A Ford owned by my pal Marsh Jaffray, discuss with classmates like Si Taylor (now Canada's ambassador to Japan) and Linc Alexander (yes, Ontario's lieutenant-governor) how we planned to save the world.

Or, we could go to the Rec Hut and watch Eric Murray cream everyone at bridge.

There were options.

In any case, they were happy times. Of course, we all complained, but it was a great time in life.

I don't know why I thought of it today, except for the fact the calendar says it's June and students are looking for summer jobs.

Ugh!

Well, all I can wish the kids is that they find their own George Oldham.

And, employers, be nice to the kids.

I've been in the full-time work force for 41 years and sometimes it still scares me.

So be gentle.

June 17, 1991

A question of etiquette, or much ado about muffin?

I've been reading the *Star* for decades and watched Canada's biggest daily go at thousands of issues head-on — separatism, scandal in the church, Brian, the plight of the farmer, sex.

Even whether the toilet seat should be left up or down.

But there is one subject the *Star* has never dared tackle.

Muffin etiquette.

Millions of muffins are consumed in this nation every day. Carrot muffins, blueberry muffins, raspberry muffins, old-fashioned bran muffins.

But not once in my many years of readership have I ever

read the proper way to eat a muffin.

More particularly, I have never spotted so much as a paragraph on how a muffin should be divided.

Of course, there are two schools of thought.

Those who feel a muffin should be cut vertically into two halves, and buttered accordingly.

And those who believe a muffin should be cut horizontally, the cap of the muffin being separated from the stem or main section.

Let me state right now I subscribe to the latter muffin philosophy.

I break off the top in one piece. Usually with my hands, not a knife.

That is because the top of the muffin is the best part and I like to keep it in one piece.

But do I do it right?

It's fine for me to take muffin in hand at home and rip off the top.

What about in polite company?

Is the vertical division the method approved by the *Star*? Is that more democratic, more in keeping with the liberal traditions of this newspaper?

I would like to know.

What does this paper's editorial board have to say?

I know what they think about the GST, the Bank of Canada's interest policy and the dangers of a free trade agreement with the U.S. and Mexico. Terrific.

But I don't have control over those things.

Muffins are another matter.

Quite often I have lunch with columnist George Gamester from this noble journal. They are always very pleasant and agreeable.

We discuss the usual things—amusing bumper stickers, vanity licence plates, anecdotes about T.O. in pre-war days.

But then comes the hard part.

The muffin.

Sometimes we agree to share a muffin and, after we figure out who bought the muffin last time, we are faced with the splitting dilemma.

This is where I go against my instincts and cut the muffin vertically — to be perfectly fair.

But, to me, a vertically cut muffin just doesn't have the same excitement as a horizontally cut one. The top, or cap, loses something in the incision.

I would prefer breaking the muffin in what (I consider) the proper way but then, besides remembering who paid last, we'd have the added burden of remembering who got the top last.

It is too much for our poor minds.

In any case, what does the *Star* have to say about muffins, and the cutting of?

The nation wants to know.

Except Quebec, of course.

Undoubtedly they'll do the opposite.

August 9, 1991

My nose has blown it in the etiquette department

Noses run in my family.

And run, and run.

From the size of it, you'd think my nose could wipe the floor with any other nose in the nation.

Not so.

My nose isn't steel. It's polyester. Drip dry, drip dry.

I don't know why that is.

My mother (who was perfect) had a lovely nose. And my father's nose knew better than to misbehave. One of his looks would have set it straight.

But me, well, that's another matter. I have an olfactory second. The Cleveland Indians of noses. A bugle that plays only one tune—honk, honk.

In short, when they handed out noses, I must have been at the end of the line.

My nose smells.

I mean by that it is very sensitive—not as good a smeller as my father's, which could detect an onion even if my mother hid it in the basement and put a lid on it.

(My father hated onions and wouldn't allow them in our house.)

No, I have no complaints when it comes to sniffing qualities. The problem is I sniff all the time.

I never go anywhere without a Kleenex in my pocket, usually two or three. There are paper hankies in my coat pockets, my tuxedo, my bathrobe. And I wouldn't think of going to bed without a box of tissues by my side.

Of course, I feel guilty. My beak has levelled more forests than the beaver.

Sorry.

But most of the time it feels as if I'm breathing through linoleum. One of my nostrils always seems shut down for repairs—sort of a Gardiner Expressway with nose hair.

In fact, when I sleep at night, I have one thumb holding open a nostril. It is a permanent pose.

What is scarier, one of my sons (Richard) is exactly the same. We are the Stuffy Twins. Between the two of us, we honk more often than Yonge Street traffic.

It drives my wife nuts. She can't understand when Rich and I sympathize with each other and complain how hard it is to breathe because of the humidity, the pollen, the heat, the cold, the front moving in from the south, the front moving in from the north.

Our sinuses aren't worth a nickel plugged.

If there is a cold virus anywhere south of Sudbury, it heads straight for my nose—unless Richard is standing next to me in which case it can make a choice.

Snort, snort, we are the losers in every nasal battle. When he was living at home, we each started the day blowing our brains out. It was really disgusting.

Throw in some wheezes, sneezes and excuse me, pleezes, and it wasn't a pretty sight, or sound.

How we got these problem proboscises, I don't know. My mother attributed it to a boyhood accident.

Once as a lad I was running full speed down the sidewalk shouting over my shoulder at a friend. I turned just in time to hit a cement pole, face first.

The cement pole won.

That may explain my problem, but why Number 2 son? Surely you can't inherit a mugging by a cement pole in your genes.

In any case, be warned.

Don't try to lead either of us around by the nose.

All you'll get for your efforts is a wet hand.

September 16, 1991

Christmas in October is not a turkey of an idea

Merry Christmas!

Ho, ho, ho, and all that festive stuff.

No, I haven't been hit on the head by a falling editor.

Nor has my brain pulled the cerebral equivalent of a hamstring.

I realize it's only October 7.

But we celebrated Christmas at our house yesterday.

We do this every October.

Of course, you're thinking of several possible reasons:

1. He thinks under the Tories the world is coming to an end so why put it off any longer.

2. He discovered documents that prove good King Wenceslaus actually looked out on the snow, crisp and even, on October 5.

3. Gift selection is much better in October.

4. The United Church has come up with another of its weird decisions.

5. He's just looking for a Monday column.

6. Nobody tracks slush into the house in October.

7. In the first week of October, no one is sick to death of Christmas carols, yet.

8. You can watch baseball on TV if the Christmas party starts to get really dull.

9. People aren't as broke in October so you can get a better present.

10. You have nearly three months to recover before New Year's Eve.

Wrong to all of the above.

We celebrate at this time of year because Jackie's parents go south for the winter and are never around December 25.

It's our last chance for a family Christmas until next April. And Christmas in April is silly.

We've been doing this over 10 years—turkey dinner, stocking presents, Christmas crackers (containing really cheap paper hats), wreath on our front door.

We don't have a tree up, of course, but Jackie hangs the usual "Merry Christmas" banner on the wall, scatters "icicles" everywhere and puts the Santa Claus ornaments on the coffee table.

We also stuff ourselves until we're semi-sick.

What could be more Christmasy than that?

This year's turkey was courtesy of son Stephen who won it at a lawyer's club dinner months ago. He claims he kept it pretty cold over the summer.

Everyone contributed something to the dinner. Of course, we boil stuff Jane brings in ever since she got the pup that licks everything, including your face.

Richard and Sirje even brought salad which, I thought, was good of them since they are still writing thank-you notes from their wedding last April.

At least that's what they claim, and that's what I told my Uncle Frank in Winnipeg who's been wondering if the gift certificate ever arrived.

I don't want you to think our Octoberfest takes all the shine out of the regular Christmas day in December.

We still have presents that can only be opened December 25.

Ted (my father-in-law) has already told us what he wants for Christmas—a bicycle helmet.

He's 77 years old and I was sort of hoping he might like a nice cardigan this year, or some rocking chair wax.

Nope, he wants the helmet.

Irene (my mother-in-law) gave him a bike on their golden anniversary six years ago and he needs the helmet for Panama City, Florida traffic.

I just hope he doesn't insist on riding granny on the crossbar this winter. We'd have to get her a helmet, too.

October 7, 1991

If not for Jackie's purse, I'd have to drop my pants

We have been in London for 10 days.

By "we" I mean the three of us—my wife, myself and my wife's purse.

I only went along for the ride.

The important travellers were my wife and her purse.

I wouldn't last 10 minutes on a trip by myself. Europe? Even Don Mills is beyond me without that magic purse.

It is black, hangs over the shoulder and contains everything a human being could ever need away from home.

Plane tickets? In the purse. Ditto passports, schedules, hotel confirmations, wheat germ pills, lemon concentrate for the tea, mints, currency in various forms, shortbreads, sewing materials, items of clothing in case of a change in weather.

If we got marooned on some lonesome road I am not certain my wife couldn't reach inside her purse and pull out a tent, a cot, makeshift plumbing facilities and two toothbrushes.

Armed with that purse, my wife could tackle anything, anywhere.

On the other hand, I'm useless—unless I can pull down my pants.

When I travel, I wear a pair of Tilley pants, the kind with the secret pocket inside one leg.

These pants are wonderful.

You can walk through a convention of pickpockets and know not a single hand will touch your valuables. Your money, papers, etc. are safer than in the main vault of the Bank of England.

The only problem is, you can't get at them either . . . unless you unzip, pull down your pants and reach inside as deep as your shoulder.

This manoeuvre isn't usually acceptable in better-class department stores or even on the street when you're trying to buy a newspaper.

Let me give you an example:

In London we saw seven plays, got Christmas puddings at Harrods, saw the Toulouse-Lautrec art exhibition, viewed the Christmas lights on Regent Street, listened to old Lord Soper handle hecklers at Speaker's Corner, dickered for Santa hats at a pushcart on Oxford Street, listened to Gershwin at a nice cafe on King's Road, viewed the royal family's art collection.

And lots more.

Not once did we have any problem. Anytime we needed anything, my wife just reached inside her purse and it appeared instantly. You can't stump that woman.

We were always on time. We never got lost. And I never had to take my pants down once.

It was only when we got back to Toronto that I ran into trouble.

At the airport we needed $20 Canadian to take the bus to the Royal York Hotel.

I had Canadian money—but down my pants.

The Resident Love Goddess merely reached into one of the 83 compartments of the purse and pulled out the $20.

"We'll need two subway tokens, too," I said, "to get home from the Royal York."

Without so much as a lousy "abracadabra," two subway tokens appeared.

Smooth? Thousands of miles and not so much as a bump.

Alas, at Union Station I pushed the subway turnstile with my bag in front of me. The bag clicked through—but I didn't.

Talk about dumb.

My wife just stared in disbelief.

I either had to take down my pants and get some Canadian money—or beg the attendant to let me through.

Happily, he heard my story and let me pass.

It was the only time Jackie's purse let me down—but you can hardly blame it for not allowing for my stupidity.

November 20, 1991

People who wear masks make me sick—I think

It is very difficult typing today.

I can only use one hand because the other's on my forehead taking my temperature. I'm also checking my tongue every 10 minutes.

I want to know if I'm sick.

Let me explain my hypochondria.

When we were waiting in the Air Canada lounge at Heathrow for our Monday flight home, I spotted a woman on a chair.

Although the lounge was crowded, the seats on either side of her were empty.

In fact, several seats both to her left and right were unoccupied.

The reason was obvious.

The woman was wearing a surgical mask. Not an itsy-bitsy mask, but one that covered her nose and mouth and did up at the back with two ties.

Since she wasn't accompanied by a horse, I quickly dismissed the idea she might be the Lone Ranger. Nor did I think she might be a terrorist, since airport security is pretty strict about letting people in masks on planes.

That left one option:

The woman had some awful disease and was really contagious.

Of course, you know what happened.

We got on the plane and discovered the woman had the seat in front of me.

I've sat on planes with bawling kids, people who threw up after too many free drinks, travellers who could talk three hours without taking a breath, etc.

But I have never sat behind anyone wearing a surgical face mask.

Frankly, I was edgy.

I do not like germs. Germs do not like me. And I swear I could see little virus things making a beeline from her surgical mask straight for me.

Wait! It gets worse.

We weren't off the ground when the woman removed her mask. Took it right off.

Then she started breathing all over the place. She even tilted her seat as far back as it would go so the germs wouldn't have to travel so far to get to me.

I couldn't believe it. (Neither could the elderly gentleman who happened to have the seat next to her. He moved over so far I thought he was going to wind up sitting on the wing.)

Why would someone wear a surgical mask in a big airport lounge and then take it off when inside a packed airplane?

For nearly eight hours she kept the mask off. She talked, laughed, ate, drank and applied smelly drops to the mask, which was tucked under her chin while we were in the air.

Okay, here's the bottom line:

When we landed at Pearson, the woman put the surgical mask back on. Yes, after we had spent all that time together, practically cheek to cheek.

When I left the plane she was in her seat, gathering her belongings—and wearing that silly mask.

I have no explanation for the odd behaviour.

I have no idea if she had the Black Death, logus-on-the-bogus, or was practising to be a surgeon.

Personally, I believe anyone wearing a surgical mask in a public place should have a cardboard sign tacked to his/her chest with an explanation.

Did I mention she had a deep-throated cough, too? Well she did.

Today I have an appointment to get a flu shot.

I just hope I've guessed right.

November 22, 1991

At age 89, Doc Lamont stops making house calls

I got a note this week from our old family doctor in Hamilton. His name is Earl Lamont and he tells me he retired on his birthday, December 3.

When he turned 89.

That's right. He's in his 90th year and has decided to turn his hand to something new—researching his family's history.

Let me admit Doc Lamont is a hero of mine.

About 50 years ago my father had some terrific pains and a doctor dismissed them as his ulcers acting up again.

The pain persisted and my mother called in a second opinion—Doc Lamont. He took one look and my father was in hospital within an hour.

Saved his life.

It was an appendix that had already burst, as they said in those days. Another few hours and he would have been a goner.

So that was the start.

Doc Lamont and his brother—they were W.E. and J.A. to patients—had an office on Main Street and were down-to-earth, no-nonsense doctors. They didn't wear shorts to the office, invite you to call them by their first name or merely direct you to somebody else for tests.

They were the real thing.

Doc Lamont delivered our three babies and one of the sweetest messages I ever got was early on the morning of December 19, 1959.

"You've got a fine son," he informed me.

If Doc Lamont said it, you knew it had to be true.

I sent Doc Lamont a picture of our three kids just a few weeks ago in a birthday card, showing how they look now.

I added jokingly, "Here are the best three babies you ever delivered."

Okay, I was serious.

Anyway, that's why he wrote back with the news of his retirement.

It was a serious blow when we moved from Hamilton and had to leave Doc Lamont. But he wasn't through with us yet.

We were living about 25 miles away when I got pretty sick one night. Well, really sick.

Jackie was all for carting me off to the nearest hospital or calling in some doctor in the new neighbourhood.

No way.

I insisted she get out the car and drive me to my mother's house in Hamilton. It was not a pleasant ride. No matter.

If I could get as far as my mother's, we could call Doc Lamont.

And he made house calls.

That's exactly what we did. Doc Lamont came over first thing and by noon I was in the hospital getting my appendix out.

As long as Doc Lamont was around, I felt safe.

So why am I telling you all this personal stuff?

Well, you read the newspaper these days and you think the world is filled with psychos, windbags, punks with guns, brutes, drug addicts, wheeler-dealers who will do anything to get an edge.

You think there are a lot of people around who just don't care.

But there are also good people.

Like Doc Lamont.

Maybe there's a Doc Lamont in your life, somebody who has made your life a whole lot better.

I hope so.

Christmas isn't a bad time to think of them.

December 13, 1991

Keep your millions of dollars —I'm already rich

I've just decided I don't want to win the lottery.

No point.

For years I dreamed of winning The Big One. You know —a cool million or two from Wintario, Lottario or some other ario.

Hip deep in $100 bills. Loonies up to the roof. Laurier's picture stuffed in every jar in the house.

Lovely.

Oh, forget it.

Just not interested anymore.

Before you think there's entirely too much aluminum cookware in our kitchen, let me explain.

The reason I wanted to win the lottery was to have a lovely villa in the south of France. Ocean view. Good bread shop at the corner. International models strolling by in swimwear by Skimpy.

It was my fantasy.

If I won a lottery, I'd make it all come true.

Goodbye daily grind, hello Côte d'Azur. Instead of putting my tootsies in fleece-lined Duckies, I'd dabble them in the Med until they got all pruney. Yum, yum.

Over the weekend I came to my senses with a thud.

I couldn't move to the south of France even if I won 10 lotteries.

Couldn't leave the kids.

To be halfway around the world from the three tykes?

Forget it.

It doesn't matter that Stephen is now 30, Jane, 28, and Richard a responsible (sort of) 26.

Couldn't leave them.

Miss my Wednesday lunches at Shopsy's with the lawyer, my Friday lunches with the only daughter, my games of catch or ice-skating sessions with the baby? Sunday dinner?

No way.

So Bardot might drop in for a cup of sugar. So the neighbour on the other side might need a companion for an afternoon sail to Nice to pick up a few things. So we wouldn't need snow tires on the family car.

Big deal.

I'd be lonely without my kids.

Is this a sign of age? Do old folks get this way?

I remember a time when we were ready to trade a piece of anatomy, your choice, for a kid-free evening.

Nobody flushing the good perfume down the toilet, or

swinging on a curtain with a towel tied around his neck, or sharing a cone with the dog on the front room carpet?

Yes, we'd have snapped up an offer of 24 hours in Detroit's inner city, provided we could go alone.

No more.

The kids are quite civilized. They have interesting stories. They wipe their feet. They buy great presents. They haven't thrown a punch at each other in years. And they hug now without leaving candy stains.

You can't believe the fuss they made over my birthday on the weekend.

If I weren't a hardened journalist with a toothpick sticking from my teeth, I could have blubbered. Especially over the card.

They have turned out really well. I can think of about 37 math teachers who would be absolutely shocked, not to mention relatives who wondered why Richard wouldn't learn to swim first before jumping in the deep end of the pool.

Anyway, cross my name off the lottery hopefuls.

I'm staying put.

November 7, 1990

I'm happy to say I'm happy

This is going to sound sappy.

But over the weekend I was thinking how happy I am.

I like my life. I like my family. I like my job. I like my country. I liked my parents. I like where I was raised. I like where I went to school.

I just like.

I'm happy.

Oh, I know there are things that are awful—disease,

hunger, war, corruption, violence.

Believe me, I don't have my head in the sand.

I worry about the state of the world, the environment, our nation, the simple lack of courtesy we extend each other.

Oh, I know all that.

But I was sitting at the kitchen table thinking about me, my years on this planet.

And I realized how happy I am.

Think I'm married to the best woman on the globe. She is funny, loving, saucy, unpredictable, loyal, hardworking, sunny in disposition, easygoing, smart, patient with me, makes a great pie and isn't all filled with herself. Also good with a buck.

You can't do better than that.

Love my kids, can't wait to see them, have lunch with them, hear their stories, listen to their ideas, travel with them. Miss them if we don't get together every few days.

Parents? Great, especially my mother. Never raised her voice to me, made me feel everything I did was important and possible, cheered me on dark days, made the greatest fried chicken in the world, had a sweet disposition, always put me first, laughed lots.

My dad worked hard, was dead honest, threw a good curve, had a deadly wit, always paid his bills, worried about spelling and quality and grooming, great poker player. Hard as nails in some ways. Moody, too. But no phony. A newspaper guy.

Which explains why I got in this business.

And what a wonderful job it is. I was an office boy (after four) in a newspaper in 1941 when I was 12. That's 49 years ago. Still can't wait for the paper to come out. Never bored with it. Love newspaper people. Well, most of them. Think it's an exciting, glamorous life. Love to say I'm with the *Star*.

Been great places. Met all kinds of people. Big shots, middle shots, little shots. Still scared every time I sit at the typewriter that it won't be good enough. That I may have it wrong.

But it's an adventure. Never dull, never the same thing two days in a row. I'm glad my one son is following in the business. He'll be good. He'll have fun.

Love this country. Boy, I'm glad my grandfather came here. I love my Austrian roots. I love to know streets in Vienna and Munich are named after Lautenschlagers. But this is Heaven. What a great country to be part of. What a great city to live in. I like it and can't think of any other place I'd want to be on a permanent basis.

A good time to be alive, too. Polio vaccine, air conditioning, jets, colour TV, the Red Cross, the Jays, OHIP, computers, French vanilla ice cream, Beethoven on CDs, reading, the Canada pension, goosedown jackets, the Sports Network, Diet Pepsi, long-distance phone calls, supermarkets, plumbing.

I'm happy.

No big complaints. Enjoyed the bumps and the good times, the good times more, of course. Wouldn't change much, if anything. Wish I were brighter, wiser and had more hair.

But all in all, I hope the next 60 plus are as good.

October 8, 1990